The God Questions
Exploring Life's Great Questions About God

The God Questions

Exploring Life's Great Questions About God

Daily Readings & Study Guide

Hal Seed & Dan Grider

"*The God Questions* is a great reminder that honest questions deserve true and thoughtful consideration. Hal and Dan have done their homework to do just that, and in the process, build the case that Biblical faith is not a blind leap in the dark, but that there are indeed some sound reasons, discernible evidences and intellectual integrity upon which to place one's personal trust in the God of the Bible."

> – Denny Bellesi, Founding Pastor,
> Coast Hills Community Church, California,
> and author of *Kingdom Assignment*

"A good question is often as important as a good answer, and *The God Questions* guides you through plenty of both. The authors weave winsome stories, expert quotes, relevant scriptures and common sense into a ready reference for both committed Christians and sincere seekers."

> – Judson Poling, editor of *The Journey Bible*

"*The God Questions* is one of the most relevant books for our day. It is practical, down-to-earth and full of helpful stories and insights for anyone who has ever asked a "God question." I love the combination of brevity and scholarship. This is an apologetics book in overalls. Anyone can benefit from it. I believe this is the book that tens of thousands of hungry people desperately need for their spiritual journey."

> – Dr. Tim Elmore, Founder, GrowingLeaders.com

"*The God Questions* is a powerful tool to help you and your friends dialogue about the deeper meaning of life. Hal and Dan have written a clear, concise and practical guide that is sure to challenge your faith and expand your perspective. Don't miss *The God Questions!*"

> – Jud Wilhite, Sr. Pastor, Central Christian
> Church, Las Vegas, and author of *Stripped:*
> *Uncensored Grace on the Streets of Vegas.*

DEDICATION

To Lori,
the love of my life.
— Hal

To Debbie,
the love of my life.
— Dan

ACKNOWLEDGEMENTS

Like most books, writing *The God Questions* was a community effort. We would like to thank Alexia Wuerdeman, Kathy Daubenspeck, Toni Ridgaway and Jennifer Dion for editing and design. Thank you also to Emily McKinley, Paul Simmons, Patty Brockelmeyer, Bob and Jan Funchess, Wava Howley, Sherry Scott, Bruce Pahl, Aggie Beane Sly, Nathan Simon and Jean Vickner for editing, proofreading and the general upgrading of the text. All of the above gave valuable suggestions. We are VERY grateful to each one of you.

Turn on the Light

Your Guide to *The God Questions* Journey

If you've ever switched on a light bulb in the middle of a dark room, you know what it feels like to be "illuminated." During the next 40 days as you explore the answers to many of life's great spiritual questions, you are going to experience mental and spiritual illumination. You are going to feel like a great big light bulb has turned on in your mind and, perhaps, another one in your soul.

The God Questions is designed to give you answers to your deepest spiritual questions. The four major and four minor questions included in this book represent most of the questions that are commonly asked about Christianity. Once you understand the answers, you will not only have the answers you need for your faith, but you'll be able to help answer your friends' questions as well.

The God Questions is written in bite-sized chunks, so that you can read for three days, meet with your small group (if applicable) to discuss what you're learning, and then read three more days to get further answers to the same general question. There is a total of 40 days, or six weeks of reading. As you read, you'll notice that Days 7, 14, 21, 28 and 35 do not have a question to address. We'd like to encourage you to take a break from your studies, or "Sabbath," on the seventh day to reflect, catch up and—we hope—attend church.

Each day's reading is short, relevant and easy to understand. Once you've read the book through (preferably with a highlighter in hand), you will be able to come back and easily find these answers again, even years from now. At the end of each chapter is a section called *"THINKING ABOUT IT."* It includes *Something to Chew On*, a *Verse to Remember*, a *Point to Ponder*, and an open section titled, *My Thoughts on the Subject*. Use this section to reflect and let what you've learned sink in deeper. If you fully utilize this section, you will find that the words you write in *My Thoughts on the Subject* will be the most important words in the book.

The God Questions was designed for study individually, with a small group or with your church as a whole. If appropriate, encourage your church to participate in *The God Questions* together. Church leader resources are available at Outreach.com. Now, let's begin!

WHAT DO ANSWERS
DO FOR ME?

"The secret things belong to the Lord our God,
but the things revealed belong to us and to
our children forever, that we may
follow all the words of this law."

Deuteronomy 29:29

Over these next 40 days, you will explore the answers to some of life's most important questions. You will acquire vital information, and information is power—especially the right information. What you are about to experience is what I call *"true truth about truth"*: not just opinion or hearsay, but time-tested and God-revealed truth. So get ready! Your new life starts today.

When I was a little guy, my father did a lot of business traveling. I loved this, because every time he came home he brought me a present. One present I remember vividly was a watch from Hong Kong. I was six years old and couldn't tell time, but I loved that watch. I wore it proudly around the neighborhood. Kids would ask me, "What time is it?" I'd say, "I don't know." And they'd respond, "What do you mean you don't know? Look at your watch!" So I'd look at my watch, but it did me no good whatsoever.

How do you suppose I felt every time that happened? Embarrassed? Yep. Stupid? A little. Lame? Definitely. I was walking around with a prized possession on my wrist, and it was functionally useless to me—until one day my neighbor Timmy taught me how to tell time! It only took a little while for him to teach me, and after that I felt empowered, important and useful. I became the time-teller for our neighborhood. Whenever any of the other kids wanted to know what time it was, they asked me.

Have you ever thought, *"I have questions about God that just never seem to go away?"* Or have you ever said, "I wish I had the answer to the questions my friends are asking about Christianity"? At the end of the next 40 days, you will be empowered to answer those questions. When you finish this journey, *"God, if you're really there, please answer me!"* The cry of every despairing hea[r] you will have more confidence in God, more confidence in yourself and more confidence in your faith, because you'll have answers to questions that have been asked of Christianity for the last 2,000 years.

Proverbs 1:7 says, *"The fear of the Lord is the beginning of knowledge."* The Hebrew word for "fear"—*Yir'ah'*—means "to shrink back in awe and lean forward in wonder." The first time I visited the Grand Canyon, I was so captured by its beauty that I instinctively leaned forward to get a better view, and instantly leaned back to keep from falling into it. That's Yir'ah. This verse also says that an important first step in any faith adventure is seeing God for who He really is. The reverse is also true: Your first steps in acquiring knowledge are the beginning of your deepening respect and reverence for God. In short, expect your sense of awe and wonder for God to grow during this adventure.

I suggest you pray this prayer as we start the adventure together: *God, teach me the answers to the questions I have about You, so that I can have more confidence and more faith.*

MAJOR QUESTION:

Is God Real?

WHERE DID THE WORLD COME FROM? *Part 1*

"The heavens declare the glory of God; the skies proclaim the work of his hands."

Psalm 19:1

Throughout human history, people have questioned the existence of God. We can't see, hear, feel, touch or taste Him, so how can we know for sure if He exists? It's such an important question that scholars have given it deep thought over the ages. Many have concluded that there are sound reasons to believe in Him. This week, we'll give you five of them; together they form a compelling argument that God is real. They'll even point you toward the kind of God He is.

Reason #1—The Universe

The universe itself is a powerful pointer to the existence of God. It's big and beautiful, and all of its parts work together well. Its very existence raises the question: *"How did the universe get here?"* Think about it: If nothing existed, would you have to explain it? Of course not! But the moment something exists, a question can be raised of its origin. Interestingly, it is the attempt to answer this question that led many scientists to conclude that God must exist.

The most obvious answer to "How did the universe get here?" is, "It came from something else." Animals come from their parents, plants come from seeds, houses come from a builder and cars come from factories. In fact, *everything* in the universe comes from something else; it is **contingent** on something that came before it.

"The first question which should rightly be asked is: Why is there something rather than nothing?" G. W. Leibniz

In addition, everything that exists depends on something else. Humans depend on food to live. Plants depend on the sun for photosynthesis. The sun depends on gravity to keep from breaking apart. So everything in the universe came from something else, and everything is **dependent** on something else in order to exist.

Push way back into the history of the universe and ask, "Where did all of this stuff come from?" The answer most people come to is "God." Everything in the universe was created by something else and depends on something else. The cause of all of this must be something that is uncreated and independent—or, in positive terms, something that is **eternal** and **self-sufficient**. The only being that could fit such a description is God.

Another way to think about this is to view the universe as one big object. Using your mind as a camera lens, zoom out so far that you capture everything in the universe in the circle below. Everything inside the circle is contingent and dependent.

THE
UNIVERSE

The universe has not always existed. Therefore, it must have come from something that is non-contingent and non-dependent. Those two terms come very close to a working definition of God.

The Bible says, "...the heavens declare the glory of God; the skies proclaim the work of his hands... There is no speech or language where their voice is not heard. Their voice goes out into all the earth, their words to the end of the world." (Psalm 19:1) God is communicating to us through what we see of the universe! He's saying, "I am here. I exist. You can tell, because I made this place."

Everything that's been made must have a maker. The French skeptic Voltaire once said, "I shall always be convinced that a watch proves a watch-maker." In the same way, the existence of the universe proves a God.

THINKING ABOUT IT

Something to Chew On:

The universe points to the existence of a Creator God.

Verse to Remember:

"The heavens declare the glory of God; the skies proclaim the work of his hands." Psalm 19:1

Point to Ponder:

When I look at the world, do I believe it is the result of intentional creation?

My Thoughts on the Subject:

WHERE DID THE WORLD COME FROM? *Part 2*

"In the beginning you laid the foundations of the earth, and the heavens are the work of your hands."

Psalm 102:25

Reason #2—The Creator

My wife and I have a very special box in a cabinet in our garage. It contains scores of pictures our daughter Amy drew as a little girl. If you look through the box, you can guess how old Amy was at the painting of each picture. Some look like they were painted by a four-year-old, others by an eight-year-old, still others by a sixteen-year-old. You can tell a lot about a Creator by studying what she (or he) has created. This illustrates the second evidence of the existence of God, although it's more subtle than the first: If there cannot be a creation without a Creator, then **every design reflects its designer**.

Chart the path of the stars, measure the decay rate of an atom, examine the laws of physics: Everything you study is well-ordered, precise and complex. Stare up into the night sky, walk along a beach at sunset, put a snowflake under a microscope; everywhere you look, our world is saturated with beauty. This beauty and complexity in the universe point not only to a Creator, but also to the nature of the Creator: ingenious, beautiful and detailed.

Plato decided that it was reasonable to believe in God based on "the order of the motion of the stars, and of all things under the dominion of the mind which ordered the universe."[1] Sir Isaac Newton said, "When I look at the solar system, I see the earth at the right distance from the sun to receive the proper amounts of heat and light. This did not happen by chance."[2]

The Pepsi Can[3]

Imagine that sitting on the desk in front of me is a Pepsi can. How did it get here?

Here's a theory: Millennia ago, a huge explosion sent a small meteor spinning through space. As it cooled, a caramel-colored, effervescent liquid formed on its surface. As time passed, aluminum crept out of the water and shaped itself into just these dimensions. Over time, this thing formed itself a one-time retractable lid, from which a crease appeared, a bit off-center, and out of it grew a pull-tab. Centuries later, red, white and blue paint fell from the sky and clung to its exterior, forming the letters P-e-p-s-i on its surface. (Obviously, these five letters have a deeper meaning to them, because you see them everywhere.)

"The mathematical precision of the universe reveals the mathematical mind of God."
Albert Einstein

This Pepsi can fits perfectly in the palm of the normal-sized human hand. Its volume is just about right for satisfying one person's desire for something sweet and liquid. It has just enough caffeine to pep you up a bit, but not so much that you realize you're actually in an artificially induced state of stimulation. Its contents are always the same. Its quality never varies.

How many scientific explanations about the nature of matter and the origins of the universe would I have to give to convince you that the Pepsi can happened by chance? What are the odds that something this complex, useful, comfortable and attractive came about as a result of a random collision of molecules? The can is too carefully designed to be the result of chance or coincidence. Some very smart people did some careful thinking and planning to make the Pepsi can happen.

The Banana

Now, hold a banana in your hand. Notice the banana fits perfectly in your palm. In fact, it fits better than the Pepsi can. It's been thoughtfully made with a non-slip surface. It comes with a time-sensitive indicator on the outside to let you know the condition of the contents before you even open it: Green means "keep going," yellow means "slow down and eat it," and black means "too late, friend."

The banana's top contains a pull-tab for convenient opening. Pull back firmly on the tab, and it peels neatly according to its pre-made perforations. If it's at just the right stage for eating, it even gives off a little "click" sound as it's opened. The wrapper peels into four pieces and hangs gracefully over your hand. Unlike the Pepsi can, this wrapper is environmentally sensitive, made completely of bio-degradable substances that in time enrich the soil it nestles in. If left uneaten, it has pre-programmed orders to reproduce itself into a whole new fruit-bearing plant, so it is a virtually inexhaustible food-producing source.

The fruit is the perfect size and shape for the human mouth, with a point on the top for easy entry. It is full of bodybuilding calories and is easy for the stomach to digest. And the Maker of the banana has even curved it toward the face to make the whole eating experience easier and more pleasant.

No wonder the Bible says about God, *"Your workman-ship is marvelous..."*[4] From looking at the design of the banana, I conclude that there is a God; that He is brilliant, creative and thoughtful; and that He loves to delight people through all five of our senses.

THINKING ABOUT IT

Something to Chew On:

The beauty, size, intricacy and wonder of the universe point to a God who loves beauty and is big, smart and wonderful.

Verse to Remember:

"In the beginning you laid the foundation of the earth, and the heavens are the work of your hands." Psalm 102:25

Point to Ponder:

What's the right response to a God who so carefully constructed the banana (and the world) for my pleasure?

My Thoughts on the Subject:

_____

_____

_____

_____

_____

_____

_____

WHY IS THERE MORALITY?

*"Indeed, when Gentiles, who do not have the law,
do by nature things required by the law,
they are a law for themselves, even though
they do not have the law, since they show that the
requirements of the law are written on their hearts,
their consciences also bearing witness, and their
thoughts now accusing, now even defending them."*

Romans 2:14-15

Reason #3—Our Sense of Morality

When I was a small child, my mother and I had a tradition. We would go to the store together, and if I was a good boy, she would buy me a treat. One of the saddest days of my young life was the day that didn't happen. I remember it vividly. We were standing in the checkout line and I put my candy bar on the conveyor belt.

"No," she said, "I'm not buying you a treat today."

"Why not? I've been a good boy."

"I'm just not, that's all."

Since she had no good reason *not* to get me the candy bar, I saw no good reason not to get it for myself. I pretended to take it back to the candy aisle, but on the way, I buried it deep in my pants pocket.

Can you guess why I remember that day so vividly? Yep, I got caught. When we got home, I snuck into the living room, pulled out my candy bar and started eating. My mother, who always seemed to have a sixth sense of some kind, found me there with a wad of chocolate in my cheek.

"What are you eating?" she asked.

"A candy bar."

"And where did you get it?"

"At the grocery store."

"And how did you pay for it?"

"I didn't."

What followed was a lesson I will never forget. Mom drove me back to the store, located the store manager and made me admit my theft, apologize and pay for the candy bar. I felt embarrassed, humiliated and ashamed all at the same time.

Did I learn my lesson? Yes and no. Yes, I learned that crime doesn't pay. But no, I didn't learn to be absolutely honest from that day forward. The truth is, when I took that candy bar, I *already* knew that I was taking something that didn't belong to me. I knew what I was doing was wrong, but I did it anyway.

I've even done it since then. I haven't stolen any more candy bars, but I have taken things that didn't belong to me. And I've done worse. I've said things that weren't true in order to make myself look better. I've done things to other people that I knew would hurt them. I strongly identify with the Apostle Paul: *"I don't understand*

> "If no set of moral ideas were truer or better than any other, there would be no sense in preferring civilized morality to savage morality, or Christian morality to Nazi morality. The moment you say one lot of morals is better than another, you are in fact measuring them by an ultimate standard." C.S. Lewis

*myself at all, for I really want to do what is right, but I don't
do it. Instead, I do the very thing I hate. I know perfectly
well that what I am doing is wrong... But I can't help myself..."*[5]

I've taken surveys in my church asking, "How many
of you have never said anything that you knew wasn't true
or taken something that doesn't belong to you?" No one
has raised their hand. We're all guilty. We all have a moral
standard that we believe in but can't seem to live up to.
Paul says, *"It seems to be a fact of life that when I want to
do what is right, I inevitably do what is wrong."*[6]

How many times have you started to do something,
and an alarm in your head said, "Don't do that!" but you
did it anyway? How many times have you opened your
mouth, and your conscience said, "Don't say it!" but you
said it anyway? You know what the right thing is, even
if you don't always do it. Where did that sense of "right"
come from? This is the third reason to believe in God: **We
all have a moral standard that is higher than we are**.

Ethical codes vary from person to person and culture
to culture, but every human being has an innate moral
standard. Where did this moral standard come from?
Since it's impossible to invent something that is greater
than we are, there must be a moral Creator who put this
standard in us.

THINKING ABOUT IT

Something to Chew On:

My personal moral standards point to an absolute Moral Standard-Giver.

Verse to Remember:

"God's law is written within them, for their own consciences either accuse them or tell them they are doing what is right." Romans 2:15, NLT

Point to Ponder:

What would the world be like without a universal sense of right and wrong? What has happened, historically, when morality has been abandoned?

My Thoughts on the Subject:

_____

_____

_____

_____

_____

_____

_____

WHO IS JESUS?

*"The Son is the radiance of God's glory
and the exact representation of his being..."*

Hebrews 1:3

Reason #4—Jesus

One of the greatest evidences of the existence of God is **the life of Jesus Christ**. Jesus claimed to be God.[7] Many people struggle with this claim, because there are only two possibilities for it: Either it's true, or it's not true. If it's true, He is Lord and God. If it's not true, there are only two possibilities. One is, His claim was false, and He knew it. The other is, His claim was false, and He didn't know it, but actually thought He was God. If it was false and He knew it, that would make Him a **liar**. If it was false and He didn't know it, that would make Him a **lunatic**. (Any person who really believes he is God must be clinically insane.) This is what's known as "The Trilemma."[8] It presents us with three choices—Jesus was the Lord, a liar or a lunatic.

C.S. Lewis, who was once an avowed agnostic, saw the reasoning behind this and eventually became a Christian as a result. Afterward, he wrote:

> *A man who was merely a man and said the sort of things that Jesus said would not be a great moral teacher. He would either be a lunatic—on a level*

with a man who says he is a poached egg—or else he would be the Devil of hell. You must make your choice. Either this man was, and is, the son of God: or else a madman or something worse.[9]

Mohammed and Joseph Smith claimed to be prophets. Buddha and Confucius were silent on the idea of God. Only Jesus claimed to be God in the flesh.

Most people who dismiss the resurrection of Christ do not take the time to look closely at the facts. But those who honestly study this unique event in history conclude, like C.S. Lewis, that no one but God Himself could pull off such a miracle. So consider the following Biblical account of the facts, corroborated by the historical knowledge of ancient Roman practices and other first century records.

On Good Friday, Jesus was flogged 39 times with a cat-o-nine tails.[10] This process was so injurious that by the time it was over, His flesh was in ribbons and His organs were exposed.[11] A crown of thorns was placed on His head,[12] and a 110-pound crossbar was placed on His shoulders.[13] He was too weak from the beating to make it all the way up the hill, so a bystander named Simon of Cyrene was forced to carry the crossbar for Him.[14] He was nailed to a cross, where He was pronounced dead by a professional Roman executioner, who verified His death by piercing his heart with a spear.[15] This Centurion was so impressed with the way Jesus faced death that he remarked, *"Truly this was the Son of God!"*[16]

"Yes, if the life and death of Socrates are those of a philosopher, the life and death of Jesus Christ are those of a God." Jean-Jacques Rousseau

According to Jewish custom, Jesus' body was placed on a stone table in the burial chamber (which was a freshly prepared tomb hewn out of solid rock[17]).

He was washed with warm water and packed in 100 pounds of spices.[18] His body was wrapped in no fewer than three separate burial garments,[19] and a 1½- to 2-ton stone was placed in front of the tomb's doorway.[20] Pilate ordered a guard unit[21] to make the tomb *"as secure as you know how."*[22] The guards sealed the stone to the tomb[23] with clay packs and stamped it with Pilate's official signet ring. From what they had witnessed, the disciples were despondent and fearful.[24] When reports of Jesus' resurrection came in, they refused to believe that He was alive.[25]

If Jesus didn't rise from the dead, His disciples would have known it. Of the original 12 disciples, Judas Iscariot hanged himself believing that his betrayal caused Jesus' death.[26] John died in exile in modern-day Turkey. The other 10 were all put to death for their faith. Sometimes good men will die for a good cause, but how likely is it that that many would die for a lie?

Jesus' tomb had been officially sealed, and the penalty for breaking a Roman seal was crucifixion upside down.[27] Who would have the courage or motivation to do this? The huge stone covering the tomb was rolled *uphill* to open the tomb entrance. Who would have the strength and numbers to do this? The Roman guard unit was trained to hold their ground against an entire battalion. Who could have overcome them?[28] When Mary, Peter and the others viewed the grave clothes, they were undisturbed (except the face cloth, which was rolled up in a place by itself[29]). The linen wrappings were lying on the table in the form of a body, slightly caved in and empty. How did that happen?

Five people examined the tomb and found it empty on what would become the first Easter Sunday morning.[30] Over the next 40 days, Jesus appeared to more than 515 eyewitnesses.[31] These eyewitnesses were from various stations in life and various states of disbelief. But their lives were so changed that they, in turn, devoted the rest of their lives to sharing the story of Jesus' resurrection with as many people as they could reach. What can explain this?

THINKING ABOUT IT

Something to Chew On:

The life of Jesus points to the existence of a supernatural world and a supernatural God.

Verse to Remember:

"He is the image of the invisible God, the firstborn over all creation." Colossians 1:15

Point to Ponder:

Do I need more proof in order to believe in Jesus' claim to be God? If so, what questions do I need answered? If not, how will I follow Jesus today?

My Thoughts on the Subject:

WHAT ABOUT MY EXPERIENCE?

"Now I know that there is no God in all the world except in Israel."

2 Kings 5:15

Reason #5—Personal Experience

On January 20, 1971, I agreed to visit a Christian coffeehouse event with some friends, although at the time I was not a Christian. During a conversation on the way there, one of my friends, Dick Roth, used a phrase I thought was really odd. He said, "I talked to God this morning." It seemed so absurd to me that I laughed out loud. However, two hours later on the way home, Dick asked me if I wanted to begin a personal relationship with God. I did! What happened to me? **I had an experience with God** at that coffeehouse. I saw evidence of His real presence in the lives of the people there. And I experienced His presence for myself, personally.

The whole idea of having a relationship with God was so new to me that when I woke up the next morning I had to verify it. So I asked the question I've asked many times since: "God, are you really there?" As I said that, I suddenly had a sense that He was saying, "Yes, I'm here." I even felt subtle chills run down my spine. I have asked that same question hundreds of times since then, and every time I ask, I get the same response: "Yes, I'm here," and I get chills. That's been happening now for 33 years.

How do I explain that? Some might say, "Well, you just really *wanted* to believe." But I really didn't. I was content with my life. However, I experienced enough evidence that night to convince me that there was a God, a God who was interested in having a relationship with me. So I invited Him to be my friend and leader, and the minute I did, I experienced Him.

The Bible says that everyone can have an experience with God if they sincerely look for Him. *"Ask and it will be given to you; seek and you will find; knock and the door will be opened to you."* It also says that we were made to experience God, that *"God...has planted eternity in the human heart..."* [32]

Nebuchadnezzar was one of the most powerful men of the first millennium B.C. As emperor of Babylonia from 605 B.C., he built the Hanging Gardens of Babylon (one of the Seven Wonders of the Ancient World) and controlled virtually all of Mesopotamia. Nebuchadnezzar was a polytheist, believing in a whole pantheon of gods. [33] His story makes its way into the Bible because, at a critical juncture in his life, he had an experience with God that left him saying, *"Then I praised the Most High; I honored and glorified him who lives forever. His dominion is an eternal dominion; his kingdom endures from generation to generation."*

"I believe in Christianity as I believe that the sun has risen, not only because I see it, but because by it I see everything else." C.S. Lewis

In about 825 B.C., the commander of the Syrian Army was a general named Naaman. In the midst of a stellar military career, Naaman contracted leprosy. Like Nebuchadnezzar, Naaman's belief system was that of his surrounding culture. He was an animist, believing that many gods inhabited various geographic features (rivers, mountains, the sky, etc.) and performed the functions necessary for life on earth (moving the sun across the sky, making rain, etc.) Attempting to find a cure for his leprosy, Naaman ventured outside of his theological comfort zone and sought the God of Israel. God healed Naaman, and based on his experience Naaman said, *"Now I know that there is no God in all the world except in Israel."*[34]

What happened to both of these men? They had an experience with God. Experience is strong evidence of the existence of God. True, it is *subjective* evidence, not *objective*; you can't replicate it in a laboratory. But even though your experience with the supernatural may differ from mine, the fact that *so many* have experienced God in a meaningful way is hard to argue with, and harder still to explain—unless God is real.

Years ago, a man named Greg started attending the church I pastor. "I'm an atheist," he announced, but he kept coming. One afternoon, after going over the evidence for God's existence, Greg said to me, "Actually, all of my life I have felt like God has had His hand on my shoulder." In their heart of hearts, most people have had that same experience. That day, Greg reached out to God just as God had been reaching out to Greg. The two of them have been doing life together ever since.

Anthropologists tell us that every culture on earth has held a belief in some type of God. But people tend to view *experience* as a weak argument for believing in God—until they reach out and have the experience for themselves. Then it becomes the most compelling reason of all.

THINKING ABOUT IT

Something to Chew On:

The experience of millions of people points to the existence of God.

Verse to Remember:

"God...has planted eternity in the human heart..." Ecclesiastes 3:11, NLT

Point to Ponder:

How have I experienced God? And if I haven't experienced Him, am I open to that experience?

My Thoughts on the Subject:

IS THERE ANY PROOF I CAN TOUCH?

"Faith is the confidence that what we hope for will actually happen; it gives us assurance about things we cannot see."

Hebrews 11:1, NLT

Even in matters of faith, we want proof. In December 2002, Cliffe Knechtle and Dr. Michael Newdow held a nationally broadcasted debate. Knechtle is a Christian pastor and a staff member at Intervarsity Christian Fellowship for college students. Newdow is an atheist attorney and physician. Newdow had recently gained national notoriety for suing to have the words "under God" removed from the U.S. Pledge of Allegiance. The subject of the debate was *"Is God Real?"*

Several times during the debate, Knechtle referred to the evidences that we have already explored in our reading. None of them convinced Newdow. Newdow consistently cited the one reason that kept him from believing: He could not see, hear, touch, taste or smell God; he had never seen God respond to a prayer like, "God, if you're real, show me a sign." Newdow was holding out for *scientific proof* for the existence of God. "If I can't see Him, I can't believe in Him," he reasoned.

Is his request reasonable? Yes and no. Yes, it is reasonable to expect evidence for the things we believe. In a court of law, no one is convicted based on hearsay; substantiated proof is required. But no, wanting scientific proof is not reasonable in a case like this, because this is not a case where science is of most help to us. Scientific proof is based on replicating a process or event multiple times in a controlled environment. Science is based on a belief that *natural laws* are always at work, so that every time we do the same experiment, we should get the same results. The problem is that God isn't merely *natural*; He's *super*natural.

Suppose a careful scientist were to set up a controlled experiment to test for God. He says, "I will believe in God if, right now, He causes this cup I'm holding to disappear," and the cup disappears. Then what? If he genuinely believes that supernatural phenomena are impossible, he will look for an explanation for the cup's disappearance that doesn't include God. His explanations might include, "Someone was playing a trick on me." "The cup never actually was there." "The cup still is there, and my mind is playing tricks on me."

"The solution of the riddle of life in space and time lies outside space and time." Ludwig Wittgenstein

Suppose this scientist really does conclude that the cup has disappeared? If he's like most of us, five minutes after its disappearance he's going to say, "Could that have really happened?" Based on the scientific principle of uniformity of results, he'll re-run the experiment to verify it. So suppose God makes the second cup disappear too? The scientist then publishes his results and others replicate the experiment in their own labs. If the cup doesn't disappear for these scientists, scientist #1 is declared a nutcase, and the whole thing is forgotten. If the cup disappears each and every time, the scientific community declares that there is a natural phenomenon to account for it and begins developing a new theory of the universe to explain it.

Physical science, by its very nature, can't verify the existence of a spiritual or supernatural being. *Reason, history* and *experience* are the only truth-tests that can be applied in a search for a spiritual being, because God Himself is reasonable, claims to have appeared in history and can be experienced by people.

I Get to Use My Brain

As we've previously referenced, the God who created human intellect did not ask us to leave it at the door when it comes to believing in Him. God has scattered evidence of Himself all throughout the world, so no one has to express *blind faith* in God or even merely *sincere faith*. The Bible indicates that, while on earth, humans have a limited capacity to perceive the spiritual realm, but one day we will be able to fully grasp it. It says, *"Now we see but a poor reflection as in a mirror; then we shall see face to face."* [35]

What's at Stake?

Some people seem to have a strong desire to believe in God. They want assurance that they're not alone in the universe. Other people have an equally strong desire to *not* believe in God. The thought of an all-powerful Creator cramps their style. But if there really is a Creator to this universe, then it's His property. In fact, we are His property.

When I was a little guy, my parents built a swimming pool in our yard. Whenever the pool deck got wet, it got slippery, so my parents made up a rule to keep us safe: *No running on the pool deck*. The rule wasn't just for family members; it was for our guests as well. In all our years of having guests over, no one ever objected to my parents' rule. Why? It was their pool. They built it, they maintained it, and they *owned* it. People knew intuitively that an owner has the right to make reasonable rules and expect guests to follow them.

The decision to believe or not believe in God should not be based on a vested interest. It ought to be based on evidence, experience and reason. How objective are you about weighing the evidence for and against God? The Bible says, *"For ever since the world was created, people have seen the earth and sky. Through everything God made, they can clearly see his invisible qualities—his eternal power and divine nature. So they have no excuse for not knowing God."* [36]

The Nature of Faith

All humans exercise faith: all humans, all day, every day. When the alarm goes off in the morning, we get up believing that we still have a job to go to. We brush our teeth, believing that it will keep our teeth healthy and alleviate bad breath. At the office, we trust our weight to the chair, believing that it will support us, just like it always has. A client asks a question and we answer it, believing that we understood the question correctly. All human experience is based on faith. We have no absolute assurance of anything, *only belief based on evidence.*

So, when it comes to believing in God, where does the majority of the evidence point? To summarize this week's readings:

- A creation requires a Creator.

- An intelligent design requires an Intelligent Designer.

- A sense of moral standards indicates that there must be a Moral Standards Giver.

- The evidence for Christ's deity says there must be a Deity.

- My personal experience tells me there is a God who loves me.

Is God real? The Bible says, *"Only fools say in their hearts, 'There is no God.'... The Lord looks down from heaven on the entire human race; he looks to see if anyone is truly wise, if anyone seeks God."*[37] If this is true, if there really is a God, then He is here with you now.

THINKING ABOUT IT

Something to Chew On:

Everything I do in life, I do by faith.

Verse to Remember:

"What is faith? It is the confident assurance that what we hope for is going to happen. It is the evidence of things we cannot yet see." Hebrews 11:1, NLT

Point to Ponder:

Many of my questions have been answered, but can I ultimately embrace Christianity by faith?

My Thoughts on the Subject:

_____

_____

_____

_____

_____

_____

Sabbath

A Day of Rest

I have found that the best way to digest good material is by switching gears and taking breaks occasionally. Today is one of those days. Ideally, this seventh day of your study falls on Sunday. If so, I recommend you attend a church service today and see what you experience there about the existence of God. See you tomorrow.

END NOTES

WHERE DID THE WORLD COME FROM? Part 2

1. William Craig, *Reasonable Faith: Christian Truth and Apologetics* (Wheaton: Crossway, 1994), 84.
2. Quoted in *Heroes of History* (W. Frankford, Ill.: Caleb, 1992), 434.
3. This analogy is adapted from Ray Comfort's *God Doesn't Believe In Atheists* (South Plainfield, NJ: Bridge Publishing, 1993), 15-17.
4. Psalm 139:14, NLT.

WHY IS THERE MORALITY?

5. Romans 7:15-17, NLT.
6. Romans 7:21, NLT.

WHO IS JESUS?

7. Jesus made verbal claims to be both Messiah and God. And He made many deliberate non-verbal demonstrations that He was God. See, for instance Matthew 12:6; 16:16-17; 21:15-16; 23:37; 28:18; Mark 2:1-2;10:18; 14:53-65; John 4:25-26; 8:58-59.
8. This argument has been popularized by Josh McDowell, *A Ready Defense* (Nashville: Thomas Nelson Publishers, 1993), 241-245.
9. C.S. Lewis, *Mere Christianity* (New York: MacMillan Publishing, 1960), 40-41.
10. John 19:1
11. McDowell, *A Ready Defense*, 222, cites the following expert description: *"The heavy whip is brought down with full force again and again across [a person's] shoulders, back and legs.... The small balls of lead first produce large, deep bruises, which are broken open by subsequent blows. Finally the skin of the back is hanging in long ribbons and the entire area is an unrecognizable mass of torn, bleeding tissue. When it is determined by the centurion in charge that the prisoner is near death, the beating is finally stopped."*
12. John 19:2.
13. John 19:17.
14. Mark 15:21.
15. John 19:34.
16. Matthew 27:54, NAS.
17. Matthew 27:60; John 19:41.
18. John 19:39.
19. McDowell, *A Ready Defense*, p. 225.
20. Mark 15:47.
21. Matthew 27:65.
22. Matthew 27:66—A Roman guard unit consisted of 16 men; each was trained to protect the six square feet in front of them. Together they were expected to hold 36 yards against an entire battalion. Four men were stationed directly in front of the object they were protecting, with the other 12 asleep in a fan shape in front of them, with heads pointed in. To pierce this defense, thieves would first have to walk over the sleeping guards, then confront the four fully armed soldiers. Every four hours a fresh set of four men were awakened and rotated to the direct-guard position.
23. Matthew 27:66.
24. Mark 16:3; John 20:11.
25. Mark 16:11; John 20:13, 20:25.
26. Matthew 27:5.
27. McDowell, *A Ready Defense*, 231.
28. McDowell, *A Ready Defense*, 234. Note: some people choose to believe that the guards fell asleep, or went AWOL. The penalty for either offense was death.
29. John 20:67.
30. Matthew 28:1-6; Mark 16:1-6; Luke 24:1-6; John 20:1.
31. Mark 16:1; Luke 24:13-18, 24:36-39; John 20:10-18, 19-20, 26-28; 1 Corinthians 15:3-6.

WHAT ABOUT MY EXPERIENCE?

32. Ecclesiastes 3:11, NLT.
33. Daniel 4:34.
34. 2 Kings 5:15.

IS THERE ANY PROOF I CAN TOUCH?

35. 1 Corinthians 13:12.
36. Romans 1:20, NLT.
37. Psalm 14:1, 2 NLT.

MAJOR QUESTION:
Is The Bible True?

WHERE DID THE BIBLE COME FROM?

"The law of the Lord is perfect."

Psalm 19:7

The Bible is not a mysterious book. It *contains* mysteries, but once you know how it is laid out, the book itself is not mysterious.

The Bible is a Collection

Technically, the Bible is not a book; it is a book of books. It's a compilation of 66 different books written over a period of 1,500 years, in three different languages, on three different continents, with consistency of message and without contradictions. The books of the Bible are ordered as follows:

OLD TESTAMENT		
HISTORY	**POETRY**	**PROPHECY**
Genesis	Job	Isaiah
Exodus	Psalms	Jeremiah
Leviticus	Proverbs	Lamentations
Numbers	Ecclesiastes	Ezekiel
Deuteronomy	Song of Songs	Daniel
Joshua		Hosea
Judges		Joel

OLD TESTAMENT _CON'T_		
HISTORY	**POETRY**	**PROPHECY**
Ruth		Amos
1 Samuel		Obadiah
2 Samuel		Jonah
1 Kings		Micah
2 Kings		Nahum
1 Chronicles		Habakkuk
2 Chronicles		Zephaniah
Ezra		Haggai
Nehemiah		Zechariah
Esther		Malachi

NEW TESTAMENT			
HISTORY	**LETTERS**		**PROPHECY**
	FROM PAUL	**FROM OTHERS**	
Matthew	Romans	Hebrews	Revelation
Mark	1 Corinthians	James	
Luke	2 Corinthians	1 Peter	
John	Galatians	2 Peter	
Acts	Ephesians	1 John	
	Philippians	2 John	
	Colossians	3 John	
	1 Thessalonians	Jude	
	2 Thessalonians		
	1 Timothy		
	2 Timothy		
	Titus		
	Philemon		

Open a Bible to its Table of Contents, and you'll see it is divided into two major sections: The Old Testament with 39 books, and the New Testament with 27 books. The Bible is further divided into types of literature. The Old Testament has three sections, containing *history* (Genesis through Esther), *poetry* (Job through Song of Songs) and *prophecy* (Isaiah through Malachi).

> "There exists no document from the ancient world witnessed by so excellent a set of textual and historical testimonies, and offering so superb an array of historical data on which an intelligent decision may be made." Clark Pinnock

The Jews (including Jesus) often referred to their Bible as "the Law, the Prophets and the Psalms"[1] reflecting these three sections, or often just as "The Law and the Prophets."[2] The New Testament also contains three sections: *history* (Matthew through Acts), *letters* (Romans through Jude) and *prophecy* (the book of Revelation).

Who Wrote the Old Testament?

The earliest-written book in the Bible is probably the book of Job. Some scholars believe Job lived as early as 1900 B.C., in which case the Bible's authorship actually spans a full 2,000 years. Job's closest rival for first-authorship would be Moses, who recorded the history of the people of Israel around 1400 B.C. The first five books of the Bible are called "The Books of Moses," though Moses could not have written the final few verses of Deuteronomy, as they describe his death and succession. (Joshua probably wrote the ending as a tribute to his leader.) Moses most likely copied the first 11 chapters of Genesis from a previous source. At the very least, the entire book of Genesis would have existed in the oral teachings of the Hebrews long before Moses was born.

Interestingly, during the late 1800s, skeptics of the Bible claimed that Moses could not have written these books, because *writing* wasn't invented until after his death. This caused quite an embarrassment in 1901 when J.D. Morgan and V. Scheil excavated the ancient city of Susa and discovered the *Code of Hammurabi* etched in a stone tablet. Hammurabi lived in 1795 B.C.

Deuteronomy 31:26 tells us that, when the Tabernacle was first constructed, the writings of Moses were placed inside the Ark of the Covenant[3] in a sacred room called the Holy of Holies. As more Scriptures were produced, they were placed here as well. Later, when the new Temple was built in Jerusalem, the Ark and the Scriptures were moved there.

Joshua deposited the book that bears his name.[4] Samuel wrote "...on a scroll and deposited it before the Lord,"[5] as well, including the books of Judges, Ruth and most of the first book of Samuel. Samuel, the last of Israel's judges and first of the line of prophets, established a school of prophets[6] who carried on his work of recording the history of God's people. These writers included Nathan and Gad,[7] Ahijah and Iddo,[8] Jehu,[9] Isaiah[10] and others.[11]

Scholars believe that Jeremiah was the prophet who completed the books of Kings,[12] along with the book of Lamentations and the book that bears his name. Ezra the scribe compiled the books of Chronicles for the benefit of the Israelites, who returned to the land following their exile to Babylon. More than half of the Psalms are attributed to King David. King Solomon wrote the books of Ecclesiastes, Song of Solomon and most of Proverbs. According to the Talmud (the authoritative Jewish commentary on the Old Testament) and the first century historian Josephus, the succession of the writing prophets ended in Nehemiah's day, with the final prophet being Malachi.[13]

The Old Testament Scriptures produced after the Temple was built in Jerusalem were kept together in the Ark. During the time of the exile in 586 B.C., the Temple was destroyed and the original copies lost forever. The scrolls used in producing today's Bible translations are copies that were in circulation at the time the originals were lost.

Thus, the Old Testament was completed about 400 B.C. This begins what is known as "the 400 years of silence."[14] Much of what happened in Israel during this "Intertestamental Period" (time between the two testaments) was written down, but there were no authoritative prophets, so the writings of this period do not bear the marks of canonicity.[15] In other words, these writings do not have the authority and inspiration of Scripture.

Who Wrote the New Testament?

Almost half of the New Testament's 27 books are letters written by the Apostle Paul as a means to instruct Christians and young churches how to live the Christian life.[16] One of Paul's close followers, the Gentile doctor Luke, wrote Luke and Acts. The Apostle John wrote five New Testament books (1-3 John, the Gospel of John and Revelation). Two were written by Peter, and one by his close follower, Mark.

Of the remaining four books, one was written by the Apostle Matthew, and two others by Jesus' half-brothers, James and Jude. The book of Hebrews is actually a sermon preached somewhere in a local church. Its authorship has been widely debated; some believe it was a sermon of Paul's, while others say it came from Apollos. One intriguing theory is that it was written by Priscilla, a female leader of the early church, who did not identify herself to keep the book from suffering gender-bias. The New Testament was completed between A.D. 46 and 90.

So What?

Ephesians 2:20 says that the Christian church is "built on the foundation of the apostles and prophets..." The Bible claims authority based on many factors we will explore this week, and the first of these is the **authorship factor**. Each of the 66 books of the Bible was written either by a prophet (someone who heard from God, whose credentials were recognized and affirmed by their contemporaries and by history), or by an apostle (one who had been an eyewitness of the risen Christ), or someone with direct linkage to one or the other.

THINKING ABOUT IT

Something to Chew On:

Every author of every book of the Bible is a trusted, time-tested, spiritual giant.

Verse to Remember:

"...built on the foundation of the apostles and the prophets, with Christ Jesus himself as the chief cornerstone."
Ephesians 2:20

Point to Ponder:

Either the Bible is true, or it is a hoax. How likely is it that 40 of history's most respected people, working over a 1,500-year time span, writing in different moods, situations and languages, collaborated on a hoax that has fooled much of mankind for most of the last 2,000 years?

My Thoughts on the Subject:

_____

_____

_____

_____

_____

_____

HOW IS THE BIBLE DIFFERENT FROM OTHER BOOKS?

*"Your laws endure to this day,
for all things serve you."*

Psalm 119:91

The Bible is unlike any other book in the world. It was the first book printed on a printing press. In fact, Johann Gutenberg invented the printing press specifically to produce copies of the Bible. It is also the most expensive book in the world. Greatsite Marketing's website offers one "leaf" of an original Gutenberg Bible for the asking price of $79,000. It estimates the worth of a complete 1455 edition at $100 million.[17] The Bible was also the first book translated into another language. (Greek-speaking Jews translated it from Hebrew to Greek in the third century B.C.) The longest telegram in history is the Revised Version of the New Testament, sent from New York to Chicago.[18] The largest first edition printing of any book in history was a Bible; 1.2 million copies were made, and the entire run sold out before printing![19]

The Bible is Unique

The 1960s were turbulent times for the United States. The young Baby Boomer generation was questioning not only the Vietnam War, but everything authoritative, traditional or created by the "establishment." During this time, a young former atheist by the name of Josh McDowell stepped onto college campuses. In his personal quest for truth, McDowell did research into the Bible. He finally concluded that the Bible is the most unique piece of literature in all of history. McDowell's lectures on college campuses drew tens of thousands of students and faculty. The outline of his message was very simple: The Bible is unique in its *continuity, circulation, translation, survival* and *teachings*. His main message to audiences: *"If you are an intelligent person and you are searching for the truth, you will read this one book that has drawn more attention than any other."* [20]

> *"It isn't the parts of the Bible that I can't understand that bother me, it is the parts that I do understand."* Mark Twain

Unique in Its Continuity

As we mentioned, the Bible was written across continents and in multiple languages over a span of well over a millennium. The diversity of its 40 contributing authors includes poets, peasants, philosophers and kings writing in a variety of moods ranging from the thrill of victory to the agony of defeat. Yet it remains consistent in its message and has no contradictions. No other book can boast this.

But the most impressive thing about the Bible's continuity is its unity. The Bible addresses hundreds of controversial issues, yet agrees substantially from cover to cover. And, in spite of the differing circumstances under which the books were written, one theme progressively unfolds from one book to the next: God's building of community with mankind. Can you imagine picking 40 authors today, all from the same time period, all speaking the same language, all writing on the same topic, and having them all agree on even *one* controversial issue—say, embryonic cell research? Or premarital sex? Or the war on terrorism? Could you even ask them to write a coherent essay together on one theme? Such a book seems impossible.

Unique in Its Circulation

The Bible is the best-selling book of all time. It has been the best-seller each and every year since 1455 when the printing press was invented. From 1810 to 1990, the International Bible Society sold or gave away 300 million Bibles in 450 languages. Since 1981, 150 million copies of the Bible have been purchased. In the weeks following the attacks of September 11, 2001, 800,000 copies were donated and distributed throughout the New York City area.[21] In 2003 alone, the United Bible Society sold or gave away 21.4 million Bibles, 14.4 million New Testaments, and 400 million selected Scriptures—over *430 million* in total.[22] What other book comes close to this kind of circulation?

Unique in Its Translation

As of 2003, portions of the Bible have been translated into more than 2,500 languages, representing over 90% of the population of the earth. Currently, there are more than 500 translations in progress by linguists throughout the world.[23] What other book comes close?

Unique in Its Survival

Because papyrus, vellum and paper are all perishable, the Bible has been recopied countless times in the last 3,500 years, yet its accuracy is uncanny. Professor and apologist Bernard Ramm explains the process the Old Testament went through:

Jews preserved it as no other manuscript has ever been preserved. With their massora (parva, magna and finalis) [methods of counting] they kept tabs on every letter, syllable, word and paragraph. They had special classes of men within their culture whose sole duty was to preserve and transmit these documents with practically perfect fidelity—scribes, lawyers, massoretes. Who ever counted the letters and syllables and words of Plato or Aristotle? Cicero or Seneca? [24]

Noted apologetic author John Warwick Montgomery describes the reliability of the New Testament text this way:

To be skeptical of the resultant text of the New Testament books is to allow all of classical antiquity to slip into obscurity, for no documents of the ancient period are as well attested bibliographically as the New Testament. [25]

In addition, no other book has suffered the same kinds of attacks as the Bible. From ancient Rome to modern communism to Islamic states, the Bible has been banned, burned, outlawed and restricted. Yet, it remains the most widely circulated and read book in the world. In fact, the Bible is so resilient that people who forecast its demise usually end up as anecdotes of history. For instance, in 1778, the French skeptic Voltaire predicted that within 100 years of his time, Christianity would be non-existent. Fifty years later, the Geneva Bible Society used his house and printing press to produce stacks of Bibles! [26] In A.D. 303, Emperor Diocletian ordered that all copies of the Christian Bible be destroyed in his realm. Nineteen years later, in A.D. 322, Emperor Constantine ordered 50 copies of the Bible be made—at government expense! What other book can make such claims?

Unique in Its Teaching

The Bible is the only book that boldly exposes itself to potential disproof by making specific predictions about the future. There are more than 2,500 prophecies in the Bible; 2,000 have already come true.[27] The other 500 remain for the future.

The Bible is the only book of antiquity that teaches history with such accuracy. It presents a clear picture of tribal and family origins.

> *In Egypt and Babylonia, in Assyria and Phoenicia, in Greece and Rome, we look in vain for anything comparable. There is nothing like it in the tradition of the Germanic peoples. Neither India nor China can produce anything similar, since their earliest historical memories are literary deposits of distorted dynastic tradition, with no trace of the herdsman or peasant behind the demigod or king with whom their records begin. Neither in the oldest Indic historical writings (the Puranas) nor in the earliest Greek historians is there a hint of the fact that both Indo-Aryans and Hellenes were once nomads who immigrated into their later abodes from the north.* [28]

The Bible is the only book that treats miracles in a matter-of-fact way. Other books of antiquity describe miraculous events with flowery and superfluous language. When Moses parts the Red Sea, the Bible simply says, *"Moses stretched out his hand over the sea, and all that night the Lord drove the sea back with a strong east wind."*[29] When Jesus turned water into wine, the text says, *"Jesus said to the servants, 'Fill the jars with water'; so they filled them to the brim. Then he told them, 'Take it to the master of the banquet.'"*[30] It never even mentions the miracle, only its effect on the master of the banquet! The Bible is the only ancient book that teaches with such humility.

It also treats its heroes with disarming honesty. It tells of Abraham's lying, Moses' reluctance, David's adultery, Peter's denial of Christ, Paul's persecution of the church and even Jesus' agony in the Garden of Gethsemane. Where other books paint the best side of their subjects, the Bible deliberately shows us real human beings who struggle.

None of these unique elements prove that the Bible is true, but they offer tremendous motivation to intellectually honest people. The Bible's promise is that "...you will know the truth and the truth will set you free." [31] Its pages call out enticingly, "Come and read. There is no other book like this one!"

THINKING ABOUT IT

Something to Chew On:

The Bible is unlike any other book in the world. Its history, influence, message and unity-in-diversity put it on a shelf by itself.

Verse to Remember:

"The secret things belong to the LORD our God, but the things revealed belong to us and to our children forever, that we may follow all the words of this law." Deuteronomy 29:29

Point to Ponder:

If the message of the Bible can turn the world upside down, what can it do for me? What can it do for my neighbors? How might I help these changes to happen, first in me, then in my neighborhood?

My Thoughts on the Subject:

WHAT ABOUT ERRORS IN THE BIBLE?

"When [the king] takes the throne of his kingdom, he is to write for himself on a scroll a copy of this law, taken from that of the priests, who are Levites. It is to be with him, and he is to read it all the days of his life."

Deuteronomy 17:18-19

People ask me, *"With all of the times the Bible has been copied from one language to another, how can we really be sure what it says?"* Whenever that question comes up, my first thought is always, "If you only knew..." Our perception of history is a funny thing. Sometimes we assume that the details we don't know are unknowable. Then one day we read an article, hear a lecture or read a book, and all of a sudden, a light goes on!

The Bible is the most accurately transmitted book of all time. Its transmission from one generation to the next has been done so carefully and is so well documented, once people know the whole story, they often remark that only God could have done such an excellent job.

The Number of Translations

A common misperception is that the Bible has been translated into so many languages; it must have been translated from one language to another, then another. Like the child's game of "telephone," where a roomful of kids sit in a circle and one whispers in the ear of the next, the message gets progressively garbled as it moves from ear to ear. If the original message was, "The duck is brown," the final message becomes distorted into something like, "Danny loves Susie."

Transmitting a message from one person to another, or from one source to another, invites errors to creep in. And with the subtle shift of meaning that comes when a message is transmitted from one language to another, you can see how distorted a message could become over a 3,400-year period. This is why Bible scholars **always translate from the original languages** of Hebrew (99% of the Old Testament), Aramaic (Daniel 2:4-7:28) and Greek (the New Testament). They take great pains to ensure that the original text is the most reliable version possible.

"There is a book worth all other books in the world."

Patrick Henry

How the Old Testament Was Transmitted

Moses, the author of the first five books of the Bible, finished his writing by saying in Deuteronomy 32:46-47, *"Take to heart all the words I have given you today. Pass them on as a command to your children so they will obey every word of this law. These instructions are not mere words—they are your life!"* Over the centuries, the Jewish people were careful not only to teach the Bible to their children, but they treated the text itself like it was their life.

The Talmudim

The *Talmudim* (Hebrew for "students") shepherded the transmission of the Torah [Old Testament] from A.D.

100-500. They had great reverence for the Scriptures in their care, and as a result their process was very careful and precise. Synagogue scrolls had to be written on specially prepared skins of clean animals and fastened with strings taken from clean animals. Each skin had to contain a certain number of columns. Each column had to have between 48 and 60 lines and be 30 letters wide. The spacing between consonants, sections and books was precise, measured by hairs or threads. The ink had to be black and prepared with a specific recipe. The transcriber could not deviate from the original in any manner. No words could be written from memory. The person making the copy had to wash his whole body before beginning and had to be in full Jewish dress. The scribe had to reverently wipe his pen each time he wrote the word "God" ("Elohim") and wash his whole body before writing God's covenant name "Yahweh."

The Massoretes

The *Massoretes*, who oversaw the Torah from A.D. 500-900, adopted an even more elaborate means of ensuring transcriptional accuracy. They numbered the verses, words and letters of each book and calculated the midpoint of each one. When a scroll was complete, independent sources counted the number of words and syllables forward, then backward, then from the middle of the text in each direction, to make sure that the exact number had been preserved. Proofreading and revision had to be done within 30 days of a completed manuscript. Up to two mistakes on a page could be corrected. Three mistakes on a page condemned the whole manuscript.

These scribes treated the text so reverently that older manuscripts were destroyed to keep them from being misread. Prior to 1947, the oldest extant Hebrew manuscript was from the ninth century. The discovery of the Dead Sea Scrolls enabled us to check the accuracy of our current manuscripts against ones from 100 B.C. When we compare the 100 B.C. scrolls to our ninth century manuscripts (a 1,000 year gap), we find that an amazing 95% of the texts are identical, with only minor variations and a few discrepancies. We also have many ancient copies of the Septuagint, the Greek translation of the Old Testament dating from the second century B.C.

How the New Testament Was Transmitted

The story of the New Testament's preservation is equally impressive. Historians use three criteria to evaluate the reliability of a historical text. They look at 1) the **number** of manuscripts available (the greater the number of manuscripts, the better the ability to compare and reconstruct the original); 2) the **time interval** between the date of original writing and the date the particular manuscript was made (the shorter the time interval, the closer to the actual events and eyewitnesses, and the fewer times the manuscript would have been recopied); and 3) the **quality** of those manuscripts (the more legible the words on the page, the more accurate the reading and comparison with other texts).

So, for instance, historians have a high degree of confidence that Julius Caesar conquered Gaul, because we possess 10 ancient manuscripts of Caesar's writings on *The Gallic Wars*. We have a high degree of confidence that Socrates lived, taught and was executed by drinking hemlock because we possess seven ancient manuscripts of Plato's *Tetralogies* in which he documents the death of his beloved mentor and teacher.

Consider the following chart: [32]

AUTHOR	WHEN WRITTEN	EARLIEST COPY	TIME SPAN	# OF COPIES
Caesar	100-44 B.C.	A.D. 900	1,000 years	10
Plato	427-347 B.C.	A.D. 900	1,200 years	7
Tacitus	A.D. 100	A.D. 1100	1,000 years	20
Thucydides	460-400 B.C.	A.D. 900	1,300 years	8
Herodotus	480-425 B.C.	A.D. 900	1,300 years	8
Aristotle	384-322 B.C.	A.D. 1100	1,400 years	49

Of all ancient Greek and Latin literature, Homer's *The Iliad* ranks next to the New Testament in possessing the greatest amount of manuscript testimony.[33] Here is how it compares to the New Testament:

HOMER (ILIAD)	900 B.C.	400 B.C.	500 years	643
NEW TESTAMENT	A.D. 40-100	A.D. 125	25 years	24,000

In terms of quality of manuscripts, author and scholar Ken Boa writes, *"While the quality of the Old Testament manuscripts is excellent, that of the New Testament is very good—considerably better than the manuscript quality of other ancient documents."*[34]

So What?

By all standards of scholarly accuracy and reliability, the Bible stands head and shoulders above all other literature in history. In the entire New Testament, only 400 words are in question (0.5%). The variants for these words are so slight that no doctrine of Christianity is affected by the potential alterations in meaning.

THINKING ABOUT IT

Something to Chew On:

When we open the Bible, we are opening the most accurately transmitted book of all time. What we read in the Bible is virtually identical to what God and the Biblical authors originally wanted to convey.

Verse to Remember:

"Take to heart all the words I have given you today. Pass them on as a command to your children so they will obey every word of this law. These instructions are not mere words—they are your life!" Deuteronomy 32:46-47

Point to Ponder:

If the Biblical message is indeed miraculously accurate in its content and preservation, what kind of impact should its message have in my life?

My Thoughts on the Subject:

IS THE BIBLE TRUE?

"...there is a God in heaven who reveals mysteries."

Daniel 2:28

I have some friends who have an insatiable need for evidence. Theories, hypotheses and even logic don't move these "show me" types. They need factual proof. God understands that; after all, He wired them that way. So, for my friends and the others like them, there exists tangible evidence for the veracity of the Bible. The authenticity of the Bible gets a huge vote of confidence from three surprising sources: *science, archaeology, and prophecy.*

Evidence from Science

The Bible is not a scientific textbook, but it does describe how the universe works. Consider the following: [37]

WHAT THE BIBLE SAYS:	WHAT PEOPLE THOUGHT:	WHAT WE NOW KNOW:
Earth is a sphere	Earth is a flat disk	Earth is a sphere
Number of stars = more than a billion	Number of stars = 1,100	Number of stars = more than a billion
Every star is different	All stars are the same	Every star is different
Light is in motion	Light is fixed in place	Light is in motion
Air has weight	Air is weightless	Air has weight
Winds blow in cyclones	Winds blow straight	Winds blow in cyclones
Blood is a source of life and healing	Sick people must be bled	Blood is a source of life and healing

For centuries, scientific theory was at odds with the Genesis 1 description of the physical and biological development of Earth. Today, scientists are in substantial agreement with the initial conditions of Genesis 1, as well as with subsequent events and the order in which they occurred.[38] The likelihood that Moses, writing 3,400 years ago, could have guessed all these details is infinitesimal.

In addition to the phenomena just mentioned, the Bible describes:

- The conservation of mass and energy.[39]
- The hydraulic cycle of evaporation, condensation and precipitation.[40]
- Gravity.[41]
- The Pleiades and Orion as gravitationally bound star groups.[42]
- The effect of emotions on physical health.[43]
- The spread of contagious disease by close contact.[44]
- The importance of sanitation to health.[45]

What grade would you give a book that could do this and was completed 2,000 years ago?

Astronomer Robert Jastrow sums it up this way. *"For the scientist who has lived by his faith in the power of reason, the story ends like a bad dream... he is about to conquer the highest peak [of scientific truth]; as he pulls himself over the final rock, he is greeted by a band of theologians who have been sitting there for centuries."*[46]

Evidence from Archaeology

Starting in the late 19th century, western scholars began excavating locations throughout the ancient Near East. To date, more than 25,000 sites have been explored.[47] Discoveries from these sites provide a second piece of tangible evidence to support the trustworthiness of the Bible by corroborating Biblical accounts with archeological findings.

Excavations at the cities of Mari, Nuzi and Alalakh verify that Abraham's customs were consistent with his 18th century B.C. culture. Excavations at Hazor, Gezer, Megiddo and Jerusalem confirm the account of Joshua's conquest of Canaan, David and Solomon's building of the United Kingdom, the demise of power during the Divided Kingdom and the Babylonian Exile.

Many key discoveries have so reshaped our understanding of history that they have been given their own unique names. For instance The Moabite Stone gives us information about the reign of King Omri.[48] The Black Obelisk depicts Assyrian king Shalmaneser III's triumph over King Jehu.[49] The Taylor Prism describes Sennacherib's siege of Jerusalem while Hezekiah was king.[50] The Lachish Letters refer to Nebuchadnezzar's invasion of Judah.[51]

"Through the wealth of data uncovered by historical and archaeological research, we are able to measure the Bible's historical accuracy. In every case where its claim can be thus tested, the Bible proves to be accurate and reliable."[36] Jack Cottrell

One of the more intriguing archeological finds is John Garstang's excavation of the city of Jericho in 1930. Joshua 6:20 indicates the walls of Jericho collapsed in a way that enabled the Israelites to charge straight into the city. For years, skeptics cited this as an example of a Biblical inaccuracy because city walls do not fall outward; they fall *inward* when they collapse, leaving the town in rubble. Guess what Garstang found? The walls fell outward! This finding was so unexpected that he and two other colleagues signed a statement verifying it.[52]

According to the book of John, one of Jesus' great miracles was the healing of the cripple at the Pool of Bethesda.[53] Outside of the New Testament, no evidence had ever been found for such a pool, so skeptics pronounced John's writing inaccurate, "the obvious work of an imposter." However, in 1888 traces of the pool were discovered near the church of St. Anne.[54]

Luke, in his gospel, gets very specific with the names of rulers, officials and events, providing ample fodder for criticism. His description of an enrollment of taxpayers,[55] his listing of Quirinius as governor of Syria,[56] his identification of Lystra and Derbe as cities in the province of Lycaonia[57] and his reference to Lysanias as Tetrarch of Abilene[58] were all called into question by Biblical skeptics. However, over time each of Luke's statements has been verified by archaeological findings. Archeologist and author Dr. Joseph Free writes, *"Archaeology has confirmed countless passages which were rejected by critics as unhistorical or contradictory to known facts."*[59]

"In the crucible of scientific investigation, the Bible has proven invariably to be correct. No other book, ancient or modern, can make this claim but then, no other book has been written (through men) by God." Hugh Ross[35]

Evidence from Prophecy

From Moses to Malachi, the role of the prophet was critical to the well-being of Israel, and God wanted His people to be able to know conclusively that these men and women spoke for Him. The Bible lays out a simple test for the authenticity of anyone claiming to be a real prophet of God: 100% accuracy. *"If what a prophet proclaims in the name of the Lord does not take place or come true, that is a message the Lord has not spoken.*[60]*... A prophet who presumes to speak in my name anything I have not commanded... must be put to death."*[61]

Can you imagine the boldness of predicting the name and foreign policy of a United States president 150 years from now? In 700 B.C., Isaiah did something similar. He predicted that Jerusalem would be surrounded and its people carried into captivity.[62] His prediction was fulfilled 100 years later. Then he went one step further; he prophesied that the Israelites would return to their homeland, and the ruler who would set them free was named Cyrus. *"I will raise up Cyrus in my righteousness... He will rebuild my city and set my exiles free..."*[63] History verifies that Cyrus, the founder of the Persian empire, reigned from 559-530 B.C., and that he issued a decree in March, 538 B.C. that allowed the Jews to return to their homeland.

Ezekiel made an equally startling prediction about the city state of Tyre (in modern-day Lebanon). He prophesied that:

- Many nations would come against Tyre (Ezek. 26:2).
- Nebuchadnezzar would destroy the city (Ezek. 26:4).
- The city would be scraped bare (Ezek. 26:4).
- Fishing nets would be spread over the site (Ezek. 26:5).
- The stones of the city would be thrown into the sea (Ezek. 26:12).
- The city would never be rebuilt (Ezek. 26:14).

Here's what happened: Tyre was a city in two parts. Half the city lay on the coast, the other half on an island one-half mile from shore. The historian Josephus tells us that Nebuchadnezzar besieged the coastal city for 13 years and finally captured it.[64] Many of its citizens escaped to the island, which remained intact. Two hundred forty years later, Alexander the Great attacked the island city.[65] Alexander built a causeway from the mainland to the island, using the stones and rubble from the old coastal city as his building material. He literally "scraped away her rubble and made her a bare rock."[66] He also used ships to attack from the sea, ships manned by people from the nations he had already conquered, including 80 from Sidon, Aradus and Byblos; 10 from Rhodes; 10 from Lycia; and 120 from Cyprus.[67] The city of Tyre has never been rebuilt. There is a small town on the island today. Fisherman from the town spread and cast their nets from the barren rocks.[68]

The Old Testament contains several hundred prophesies related to the coming Messiah; 332 of these were fulfilled in Christ's first coming.[69] (We have listed 61 of them in the endnotes.[70]) Using the mathematical science of probability, author Peter Stoner, an academic in the areas of science and mathematics, calculated the odds that any one person could fulfill just eight prophesies predicted of the Messiah. After doing his calculations, he said, "...we find that the chance that any man might have lived down to the present time and fulfilled eight prophecies is 1 in 10^{17}." (1 in 100,000,000,000,000,000.)[71]

To illustrate that probability in practical terms, Stoner used the following illustration:

> Supposing we take 10^{17} silver dollars and lay them on the face of Texas. They will cover all of the state two feet deep. Now mark one of these silver dollars and stir the whole mass thoroughly, all over the state. Blindfold a man and tell him that he can travel as far as he wishes, but he must pick up one silver dollar and say that this is the right one. What chance would he have of getting the right one? 1×10^{17}.[72]

Calculating the probability that someone could fulfill 48 prophecies gave Stoner the number 1×10^{157}. The number of atoms in the universe has been calculated at 10^{66}.

THINKING ABOUT IT

Something to Chew On:

God created us with a desire for evidence of what to believe, and He has given us this evidence.

Verse to Remember:

"...there is a God in heaven who reveals mysteries."
Daniel 2:28

Point to Ponder:

What impact does this evidence for the authenticity of the Bible have on my life? Is there anyone I know who might also be interested in these insights?

My Thoughts on the Subject:

WHAT DOES THE BIBLE SAY ABOUT ITSELF?

"And the words of the LORD are flawless, like silver refined in a furnace of clay, purified seven times."

Psalm 12:6

The Bible makes bold claims about itself. It claims to be active (Hebrews 4:12), authoritative (Deuteronomy 32:46-47), enduring (Psalm 119:91), flawless (Psalm 12:6), good (Psalm 119:39), instructive (Psalm 119:24), perfect (Psalm 19:7), powerful (Jeremiah 23:29), revelatory (Exodus 24:4), trustworthy (2 Samuel 7:28) and so much more. Are these claims true?

Yesterday we looked at evidence from outside sources; today we'll look *inside* the source and examine some of what the Bible says about itself. Someone might call this circular reasoning: "You can't judge a book by what it says about itself!" But in a court of law, defendants have the right to take the witness stand and speak for themselves.

Two Claims

Let's examine just two claims the Bible makes:

1. It claims to be a roadmap for life.
2. It claims to speak to us about our inner thoughts and motives.

The Bible as a Roadmap

The Bible says in 2 Timothy 3:16, *"All Scripture is God-breathed and is useful for teaching, rebuking, correcting, and training for righteousness..."*

"Teaching" means that the Bible says to the student, "Here is the road." "Rebuking" means that the Bible says, "Oops! You got off the road!" "Correcting" means, "Here's how to get back on the

> *"One of the many divine qualities of the Bible is that it does not yield its secrets to the irreverent and the censorious."*
>
> James I. Packer

road." "Training in righteousness" means, "This is how to stay on the road." So, does the Bible fulfill these four functions?

I came to Christ when I was 13 years old. Since that time, as I have read the Bible, it has defined right and wrong, good and bad for me. It has defined the road, and it has also helped me see when I have gotten off the road. In fact, while friends and spiritual leaders have given me much input over the years, it's the words from the Bible that have most often said to me, "Oops! You're off the road!"

As the pastor of a young church, I've spent the past 12 years seeking answers in the Bible for people who have gotten off the road and want to know how to get back on. Every week I approach the Bible for these practical answers for living life, and every week I am impressed with how God thought to include the particular topic my people needed.

If the Bible always explains and/or demonstrates how to get on the road, the Bible's true forte is helping people stay on the road. I have never come across a topic that the Bible did not address, either directly or in principle. Financial difficulties? Parenting? In-Laws? Out-Laws? Sex? Abortion? Developing confidence? Handling loss? Growing old? Improving your attitude? Improving your I.Q.?

Physical exercise? It's all there and more. Granted, I can only speak from my own experience, but survey 100 serious Bible readers, and you'll find that they all agree with me. **The Bible has proved to be a roadmap for everyone** who turns to it for direction.

It Speaks to Me About Who I Am

My normal habit is to read a portion of the Bible every morning. When I do, often it induces a dialogue within me. Say I'm reading a portion of Scripture about the importance of being honest. As I'm reading, I'm thinking, *"I'm a pretty honest person. There may have been a time when I was less honest. I'm sure glad this passage isn't speaking to me."* Then a second thought comes from deeper within me: *"Actually, you're not completely honest. You want people to think better of you than you really are, so you tend to send signals or say things that lead people to think more highly of you than they should. This is something you should work on."* What happened? My thoughts were "judged" by the words I was reading. This doesn't happen to me when I'm reading a novel or watching television, but it happens regularly when I read the Bible. As I compare my experience with friends, they affirm the same thing: **The Bible speaks to us about who we really are.**

Do these two claims constitute proof that the Bible is true? No, we would have to examine the claims of hundreds of Scriptures one at a time for that. But if the Bible is true, this examination is a worthwhile endeavor—a lifelong endeavor. And it's a logical endeavor for anyone who wants divine guidance for his or her life.

Summary

In the modern age, the primary test for truth was *logic*, i.e., "Things that are reasonable or provable are true."

In the post-modern age, the primary test for truth is *experience*, i.e., "Things that work for me are true." The most convincing post-modern proof of the Bible's veracity is locked inside the heart of those with direct experience reading, interacting with and applying the Bible. Ultimately, no one can come to a conclusion about the Bible until he or she reads it.

THINKING ABOUT IT

Something to Chew On:

The Bible's claims are backed by the personal experience of millions of believers. But the ultimate proof lies in reading and experiencing it for ourselves.

Verse to Remember:

"Your word is a lamp to my feet and a light for my path." Psalm 119:105

Point to Ponder:

As I open the New Testament and read any paragraph, does it "judge" the thoughts and attitudes of my heart? If so, how?

My Thoughts on the Subject:

_____

_____

_____

_____

_____

_____

_____

WAS THE BIBLE WRITTEN BY GOD OR MEN?

Above all, you must understand that no prophecy of Scripture came about by the prophet's own interpretation. For prophecy never had its origin in the will of man, but men spoke from God as they were carried along by the Holy Spirit."

2 Peter 1:20-21

"The Bible is God's Word, but in what sense? Throughout the Bible, there are passages where the writer says, *"The word of the Lord came to me..."* or God says, *"Write down these words."* But there are other times when writers like Luke say, *"I decided to write..."* So which is it? Were the human writers passive dictation machines, or did they write what they wanted to write? Two descriptions from Biblical writers themselves help shed light on this question.

Inspiration and the Will of Man

The Apostle Paul wrote in 2 Timothy 3:16, *"All Scripture is inspired by God..."* The word "inspired" is *theopneustos* in Greek. Some versions translate it "God-breathed" or more precisely, "God-exhaled." According to this verse, that which was written by Biblical authors started in the mind of God.

Peter writes in 2 Peter 1:20-21, "... *no prophecy of Scripture came about by the prophet's own interpretation. For prophecy never had its origin in the will of man...*" Peter is affirming that each writer was moved by God to write what God wanted written.

If God directed the writing process, why aren't all the writings alike? Isaiah writes with confidence, Jeremiah with sorrow. John uses very simple Greek; Luke uses technical language. This raises three more questions:

1. Some parts of the Bible aren't original to the Biblical writers. Joshua quotes the book of Jasher in Joshua 10:13; Jude quotes the book of Enoch in Jude 14. Paul quotes a hymn written by a musician in the church in Philippians 2:6-11, and he even quotes Epimenides, a polytheist, in Acts 17:28. *Were these quotes "God-breathed" when composed by their original writers?*

2. Some portions of the Bible are written in prose that lends itself to dictation. But other portions are written in poetry (Psalms), parables (Ezekiel 24:2), riddles (Proverbs 1:6), satire (Matthew 19:24), allegory (Galatians 4), hyperbole (Matthew 5:29) and many other forms. *Why so much variety?*

3. Throughout the Bible there are descriptions that are scientifically inaccurate, like "sunrise" as in Joshua 1:15, or "from one end of the earth to the other" in Deuteronomy 28:64. *How could God use language that He knew was wrong?*

Human Agency

God intentionally allowed human agency to play a role in the style and tone of the Bible. God wrote what He wanted written through the unique personality of each chosen author. Biblical authors were not merely stenographers. In the process of inspiration, God prepared the heredity, background and time-in-history of each writer. So when writers recorded events, composed poems and wrote allegories, the words used were their personal, conscious compositions guided by the mind of God.

Truth

Why are non-Biblical sources quoted in the Bible? Joshua and the other Biblical history writers utilized historical sources *under the inspiration of the Holy Spirit* to record the truth of Israel's history. Jude used a source familiar to his audience (the book of Enoch) *under the inspiration of the Holy Spirit* to make the point that the Lord will return and judge the world. Paul used the works of others under the inspiration of the Holy Spirit to convey the messages God had for His children.

God's Creativity

So why are there so many types of literature in the Bible? God inspired a diversity of literature forms to speak to diverse people. In addition, different forms of literature serve different purposes. Stories, which make up 40% of the Bible, paint pictures in our minds, imparting lessons that attach to those pictures. Instructional literature, from the letters of the New Testament, speaks truth straight to the mind on issues like theology and behavior. Prophetic literature requires concentration to understand, forcing the mind to think deeply, while poetic literature must be read slowly to appreciate the nuanc-

"I must confess to you that the majesty of the scriptures astounds me...If it had been the invention of man, the invention would have been greater than the greatest heroes." Jean-Jacques Rousseau

es. Finally, apocalyptic literature (Daniel and Revelation) unleashes the imagination and sometimes shocks us in a science-fiction-like manner. Each literary form touches or moves us in a different way. Some literary scholars believe that the Bible is actually the archetype for every kind of literature known to man. The Bible is rich in its diversity of style and, like Creation itself, this diversity reflects the creativity of God.

In the composition of Scripture, God breathed the truth He wanted to communicate into the minds of the people He had prepared. In this way, the words, forms and concepts that were written down were fully His *and* fully theirs.

THINKING ABOUT IT

Something to Chew On:

In writing Scripture, God expressed His sovereignty, creativity and leadership by preparing and inspiring people to write exactly what He wanted written.

Verse to Remember:

"Above all, you must understand that no prophecy of Scripture came about by the prophet's own interpretation. For prophecy never had its origin in the will of man, but men spoke from God as they were carried along by the Holy Spirit." 2 Peter 1:20-21

Point to Ponder:

How is God expressing His sovereignty, creativity and leadership in my life? What might He be prompting me to do?

My Thoughts on the Subject:

Sabbath

A Day of Rest

According to the Bible (Genesis 2:3), "God blessed the seventh day and made it holy, because on it he rested from all the work of creating that he had done." Attend a Bible-teaching church today and see what you learn about the Bible's claims from what you experience there. See you tomorrow.

END NOTES

WHERE DID THE BIBLE COME FROM?

1. Luke 24:44.
2. Matthew 7:12.
3. 2 Kings 22:8.
4. Joshua 24:6.
5. 1 Samuel 10:25.
6. 1 Samuel 10:5; 19:20.
7. 1 Chronicles 29:29.
8. 2 Chronicles 9:29; 13:22.
9. 2 Chronicles 20:34.
10. 2 Chronicles 32:32.
11. 2 Chronicles 33:19.
12. Norman Giesler and William Nix, *From God to Us*, (Chicago, IL: Moody Press, 1974), p. 82-83.
13. Josephus, *Against Apion*, I. 8.
14. The Talmud records, "After the latter prophets Haggai, Zechariah, and Malachi, the Holy Spirit departed from Israel."
15. The writings done during this period in Israel are a collection of 15 books known as "The Apocrypha." They were adopted as inspired by the Catholic church at the Council of Trent in 1546, after the onset of the Protestant Reformation, but have never been recognized as such by the Protestant, Anglican, or Orthodox churches.
16. Romans through Philemon, 13 out of 27.

HOW IS THE BIBLE DIFFERENT FROM OTHER BOOKS?

17. http://www.greatsite.com/ancient-rare-bible-leaves/gutenberg-1455-leaf.html.
18. Steve Kumar, *Christianity for Skeptics*, p. 100.
19. http://www.gospelcom.net/ibs/aboutibs/historical.php.
20. Josh McDowell, *Evidence That Demands a Verdict*, San Bernadino, CA, Campus Crusade for Christ, 1972, 20-26.
21. http://www.gospelcom.net/ibs/aboutibs/historical.php
22. http://www.biblesociety.org/index2.htm
23. http://www.biblesociety.org/index2.htm
24. Bernard Ramm, *Protestant Christian Evidences* (Chicago: Moody, 1957) cited in McDowell, *A Ready Defense*, p. 30.
25. John W. Montgomery, *History of Christianity* (Downer's Grove, IL: IVP, 1971), 29, cited in McDowell, *A Ready Defense*, p. 30.
26. McDowell, *A Ready Defense*, p. 30.
27. For specific prophecies, consult www.godandscience.org.
28. William Albright, *Recent Discoveries in Bible Lands* (New York: Funk & Wagnalls, 1955), 70ff.
29. Exodus 14:21.
30. John 2:7-8.
31. John 8:32.

WHAT ABOUT ERRORS IN THE BIBLE?

32. Christian Apologetics & Research Ministry, www.carm.org.
33. Bruce Metzger, *Chapters in the History of New Testament Criticism*, (Grand Rapids, MI.: Eerdmans, 1964), p. 144.
34. Ken Boa and Larry Moody, *I'm Glad you Asked* (Colorado Springs, CO: Victor Books, 1994), p. 92.

IS THE BIBLE TRUE?

35. Hugh Ross, www.Reasons.org.
36. Jack Cottrell, *The Authority of the Bible* (Grand Rapids, MI.: Baker, 1979) 48-49.
37. Hugh Ross, www.Reasons.org.
38. www.Reasons.org (consult for more extensive descriptions)
39. Ecclesiastes 1:9; 3:14-15.
40. Job 36:27-29.
41. Ecclesiastes 1:7; Isaiah 55:10.
42. Job 26:7; Job 38:31-33. (Note: According to Dr. Ross, "All other star groups visible to the naked eye are unbound, with the possible exception of the Hyades.")
43. Proverbs 15:30; 16:24; 17:22.
44. Leviticus 13:45-46.
45. Numbers 19; Deuteronomy 23:12-13.
46. Robert Jastrow, *The Intellectuals Speak Out About God* (Lake Bluff, IL.: Regnery Gateway, 1984), p. 21.
47. Donald Wiseman (Director of the British Museum), "Archaeological Confirmation of the Old Testament," in *Revelation and the Bible*, Carl Henry, editor (Grand Rapids, MI.: Baker, 1958), p. 301-2.
48. 1 Kings 16:23.
49. 2 Kings 10:36.
50. 2 Chronicles 32:2-9.
51. 2 Kings 24:10; Ken Boa and Larry Moody, *I'm Glad You Asked*, p. 97
52. John Garstang, *Joshua Judges*, 1931, cited in McDowell, *Evidence*, p. 71.
53. John 5:1-15.

54. F.F. Bruce, "Archaeological Confirmation of the New Testament," cited by McDowell, *Evidence*, p. 75.
55. Luke 2:1-2.
56. Luke 2:2.
57. Acts 14:6.
58. Luke 3:1.
59. Joseph Free, *Archaeology and Bible History* (Wheaton: Scripture Press, 1969), p. 1. (As cited in Kumar, *Christianity for Skeptics*, p. 109).
60. Deuteronomy 18:21-22.
61. Deuteronomy 18:20.
62. Isaiah 27-32.
63. Isaiah 45:13.
64. http://ragz-international.com/chaldeansneb.htm
65. http://joseph_berrigan.tripod.com/ancientbabylon/id34.html.
66. Ezekiel 26:4.
67. John Ankerberg and John Weldon, *Ready with an Answer* (Eugene, OR.: Harvest House, 1997), p. 248.
68. Erwin Lutzer, *You Can Trust the Bible* (Chicago: Moody Press, 1998), p. 98.
69. http://www.iclnet.org/pub/resources/text/rtg/rtg-evid/rtgevd04.txt.

70. Prophecy:

Prophecy	Fulfillment
Born of a woman, Gen. 3:15	Matt. 1:20; Gal. 4:4
Born of a virgin, Isaiah 7:14	Matt. 1:18; Luke 1:26-35
Call, "The Son of God", Ps. 2:7	Matt. 3:17; 14:33; 16:16; 26:63
Seed of Abraham, Gen. 22:18	Matt. 1:1; Gal. 3:16
Son of Isaac, Gen. 21:12	Luke 3:23; Matt. 1:2
Son of Jacob, Num. 24:17	Luke 3:23, Matt. 1:2
Tribe of Judah, Gen. 49:10	Matt. 1:2; Heb. 7:14
Family line of Jesse, Isaiah 11:1	Luke 3:23; Matt. 1:6
House of David, Jer. 23:5; Ps. 132:11	Luke 3:23; Matt. 9:27
Born at Bethlehem, Micah 5:2	Matt. 2:1; Luke 2:4
Presented with gifts, Ps. 72:10	Matt. 2:1, 11
Herod kills children, Jer. 31:15	Matt. 2:16
His pre-existence, Mic. 5:2; Is. 9:6	Col. 1:17; John 1:1; Rev. 1:17
He will be called Lord, Ps. 110:1	Luke 2:11; Luke 20:41-44
He will be Immanuel, Isaiah 7:14	Matt. 1:23; Luke 7:16
He will be a prophet, Deut. 18:18 4:19	Matt. 21:11; Luke 7:16, John
He will be a priest, Ps. 110:4	Heb. 3:1; Heb. 5:5-6
He will be a judge, Isaiah 33:22	John 5:30; 2 Tim. 4:1
He will be a king, Ps. 2:6; Zech. 9:9 18:33-38	Matt. 27:37, Matt. 21:5, John
Anointed by Holy Spirit; Is. 11:2 John 1:32	Matt. 3:16-17; Mark 1:10-11;
His zeal for God, Ps. 69:9	John 2:15-17
Preceded by Messenger, Is. 40:3 1:23	Matt. 3:1-2; Matt. 11:10; John
Ministry begins in Galilee, Is. 9:1	Matt. 4:12, 13, 17
Ministry of miracles, Is. 35:5-6 John 5:5-9	Matt. 9:32-33; Mk. 7:33-35;
Teacher of parables, Ps. 78:2	Matt. 13:34
Would enter the Temple, Mal. 3:1	Matt. 21:12
Would enter Jerusalem on donkey, Zech. 9:9	Luke 19:35-37; Matt. 21:6-11
"Stone of Stumbling" to Jews, Ps. 118:22	1 Pet. 2:7; Rom. 9:32-33
"Light" to Gentiles, Isaiah 60:3; 49:6	Acts 13:47-48
Resurrection, Ps. 16:10; 30:3; 41:10 16:6	Acts 2:31; Luke 24:46; Mk.
Ascension, Ps. 68:18	Acts 1:9
Seated at right hand of God, Ps. 110:1 35	Heb. 1:3, Mk. 16:19; Acts 2:34-
Betrayed by a friend, Ps. 41:9; 55:12-14 13:21	Matt. 10:4; 26:49-50; John
Sold for 30 pieces of silver, Zech. 11:12	Matt. 26:15; 27:
Money to be thrown in God's house, Zech. 11:13	Matt. 27:5
Price given for potter's field, Zech. 11:13	Matt. 27:7
Forsaken by his disciples, Zech. 13:7; Mark 14:50; 14:27	Matt. 26:31
Accused by false witnesses, Ps. 35:11	Matt. 26:59-61
Dumb before accusers, Isaiah 53:7	Matt. 27:12-19
Wounded and bruised, Is. 53:5; Zech. 13:6	Matt. 27:26
Smitten and spit upon, Is. 50:6; Mic. 5:1	Matt. 26:67; Luke 22:63
Mocked, Ps. 22:7-8	Matt. 27:31
Fell under the cross, Ps. 109:24-25 27:31-32	John 19:17; Luke 23:6, Matt.
Hands and feet pierced, Ps. 22:16; Zech. 12:10	Luke 23:33; John 20:25
Crucified with thieves, Is. 53:12	Matt. 27:38, Mark 15:27-28
Prayed for his persecutors, Is. 53:12	Luke 23:34

Rejected by his own people, Is. 53:3	John 7:5, 48; Matt. 21:42-43
Friends stood afar off, Ps. 38:11	Luke 23:49; Mk. 15:40; Matt.
27:55-56	
People shook their heads, Ps. 109:25	Matt. 27:39
Stared upon, Ps. 22:17	Luke 23:35
Garments parted/lots cast, Ps. 22:18	John 19:23-24
To suffer thirst, Ps. 69:21; Ps. 22:15	John 19:28
Gall & vinegar offered to him, Ps. 69:21	Matt. 27:34; John 19:28-29
His forsaken cry, Ps. 22:1	Matt. 27:46
Committed himself to God, Ps. 31:5	Luke 23:46
Bones not broken, Ps. 34:20	John 19:33
Heart broken, Ps. 22:14	John 19:34
His side pierced, Zech. 12:10	John 19:34
Darkness over the land, Amos 8:9	Matt. 27:45
Buried in rich man's tomb, Is. 53:9	Matt. 27:57-60

71. Peter Stoner, *Science Speaks* (Chicago: Moody Press, 1963), cited in McDowell, *Evidence*, p. 175-176.
72. Ibid.

MAJOR QUESTION:

Do All Roads Lead to Heaven?

ISN'T "ONLY ONE WAY" TOO NARROW?

"Jesus told him, 'I am the way, the truth, and the life. No one can come to the Father except through me.'"

John 14:6 NLT

One of the most passionate questions of belief has to do with *exclusivity;* in other words, some people say Christianity is too narrow. After all, what kind of a God would limit people to just one way of getting into heaven? Shouldn't He let all well-intentioned people into heaven? Couldn't He be generous and broad-minded enough to let everyone in who tries? Aren't all religions pretty much the same when you get right down to it?

This idea has a long history. In A.D. 384, Christianity had become the favored religion of the Roman Empire, and Emperor Valentinian ordered the removal of the Altar of Victory from the Roman Senate. Symmachus, Prefect of Rome, wanted to allow continued pagan worship in the senate chambers. Notice his line of reasoning as he appeals to the Emperor: *"It is just that all worship should be considered as one. We look on the same stars, the sky is common, the same world surrounds us. What difference does it make by what pains each seeks the truth?"*[1] In effect, Symmachus was arguing, "We're all human, and we're all seeking. Isn't that what counts? Since God is so kind and understanding, aren't *good intentions* what really matter to Him anyway?"

The Problem of Good Intentions

Good intentions have gotten me into trouble more times than I care to count. When I was in college, I had the best of intentions when I dove into the pool to lead off our school's 400-yard freestyle relay at the National Championships. I was so amped up for the race that I forgot to drop my head as I hit the water. As a result, my goggles rolled off my eyes and settled around my mouth, producing drag and making it impossible to take a breath. Each time I turned my head to breath, the goggles dumped water into my mouth, practically drowning me! My good intentions helped me swim hard, but they didn't help me swim fast. Not only did I pay for that mistake, the guys on my relay team suffered too. Good intentions coupled with poor methodology still made for a bad swim, a very upset coach and several disappointed teammates. That day I learned that all my intentions can be good and sincere, but they can still be sincerely wrong.

> "To maintain that all religions are paths leading to the same goal...is to maintain something that is not true ... The only common ground is that the function of religion is to provide release; there is no agreement at all as to what it is that man must be released from. The great religions are talking at cross purposes."
>
> R.C. Zaehner

All of the major religions of the world ask their followers for sincerity. Each one also asks for *exclusivity*. Each one claims that *their way is the only way*. During this week's readings, we'll explore the claims and paths of the world's largest religions. As you read, you'll see that there *can't* be two or more roads to heaven, because not only are the *roads* extremely different, but the *destinations* don't look anything alike either. Why would God allow confusion like this? Why would a loving God visit one area of the world and describe one way to get to heaven, and then show up in another area and tell them something different? Answer: *He wouldn't.*

There is a Deceiver

The Bible says in John 8:44 that there is another force at work in this world. Jesus said, *"When he [the Devil] lies, he speaks his native language, for he is a liar, and the father of lies."* Satan is a master of misdirection and misinformation. The *last* thing he wants is for people to worship the One True Living God. So if Satan can't keep us from worshiping God, he'll deceive us into worshiping anything but God.

"Narrow" is Not Always "Bad"

Many people have felt that God is cold and narrow, because He has only allowed one way to get to heaven. One night a few years ago, I was diagnosed with appendicitis. The doctor told me that the only way to relieve my pain and save my life was to have my appendix removed. "Could it be anything else?" I asked. "Is there anything I can do to avoid having an operation?" The doctor answered, "Not if you want to live." That was a *very* narrow answer, but not once did I think he was uncaring or cold because he gave me only one option.

Is God uncaring because He only gives us one option? Consider this:[2] Suppose that once upon a time, a good and loving God created people in His own image. Suppose He gave those people free will, so that they could make their own choices. Suppose He set them up in an idyllic environment with plenty of food and sunshine and interesting things to do. Suppose He imposed one restriction on them, warning them that if they violated the restriction, they would lose the gift of life He had given them.

Suppose His creation violated that restriction for no good reason, just because they felt like it. Suppose that, instead of taking their lives, God made provision for them and forgave them. Suppose that, despite God's provision, their descendants repeated that pattern over and over again.

Suppose that God bestowed special gifts on one particular nation, so that they could know Him deeply and help others break the destructive pattern. Suppose this chosen nation rebelled, too. Suppose that, time after time, God forgave this nation, delivered them from their current debacle, and sent special messengers to communicate with them. But suppose these people killed the messengers, turning their backs on Him, inventing other religions and, instead of God, worshiping stone idols and animals and mountains and rivers and streams.

Suppose, in an ultimate act of redemption, God Himself came to them in a human body as the Son of God, not to condemn them but to redeem them. Instead of welcoming Him, suppose the people rejected, tortured and killed Him. Suppose that God accepted the death of His Son as payment for the sins of the very people who put Him to death. Suppose that God offered His Son's murderers complete forgiveness, transcendent peace and eternal life as a free gift. Suppose God said, "I demand only one thing from you in return: that you honor My Son, who gave His life for you."

If God did all this, would you still say, "God, you aren't being fair. You haven't done enough. I want another option"? The wonder is not *"Why is there only one way?"* It's *"Why is there any way at all?"*

THINKING ABOUT IT

Something to Chew On:

The wonder is not "Why is there only one way?" It's rather, "Why is there any way at all?"

Verse to Remember:

"Jesus told him, 'I am the way, the truth, and the life. No one can come to the Father except through Me.'" John 14:6, NLT

Point to Ponder:

What does God deserve from me in return for what He's done for me?

My Thoughts on the Subject:

WHAT DO MUSLIMS BELIEVE?

"Jesus said, 'You have heard it said,
"Love your neighbor and hate your enemy."
But I tell you: Love your enemies and pray for
those who persecute you...' "

Matthew 5:43-44

Islam is the world's second-largest religion with 1.5 billion followers. The Islamic population is doubling every 26 years; the world's population is doubling every 40 years. Islam has recently overtaken Judaism as the second-largest religion in America. In 2003, there were an estimated six million U.S. Jews and almost eight million U.S. Muslims.

History

Islam's founder, Mohammed, was born in Mecca near the coast of the Red Sea around A.D. 570. His family was a minor branch of a Bedouin caste of merchant traders called the *"Quraysh."* At that time, the Arab people were polytheists, believing in many gods. According to some sources, they worshiped one god for each day of the year. Allah, the moon god, was one of those. Allah's symbol, the crescent, is still seen as the chief symbol of Islam today.

One night in 610, Mohammed had a visitation from one whom he believed was the angel Gabriel. We read in the Koran that the angel told him, "In the name of thy Lord the Creator, who created mankind from a clot of blood, recite!" (Sura 96:1) Mohammed recited, then he described his revelations to his relatives and friends. He taught them that of all the gods they were worshiping, only the one they called "Allah" was the true God and demanded absolute submission to himself. In addition, Mohammed claimed that God had called him as Allah's last and greatest prophet.

> "There is no god but Allah, and Mohammed is his prophet."
>
> First of the Five Pillars of the Muslim Faith

View of God: *Monotheism*

Mohammed taught that there is only one God (Sura 2:133). He believed that Christianity's teaching of a Tri-une God (one God consisting in Three Persons: Father, Son and Holy Spirit) was a form of polytheism (Sura 5:73). Many Muslims today believe that Christianity's Trinity consists of God the Father, the Mother Mary and their Son, Jesus.[3]

Holy Book: *The Koran*

For 22 years, Mohammed recited, and the result is one of the most significant books of mankind, the *Koran* (which means, "The Recitation"). Made up of 114 "Recitations" (or chapters called *Suras*), the Koran crystallized the Arab language and spread it across much of the world. The Koran is a visionary's book, passionately conveying Mohammed's genius and intuition.

Central Teaching: *The Five Pillars*

The word "Islam" means "submission" in Arabic. A

"Muslim" is a "submitted one." The focus of Islam is submission to Allah, and the central teaching of Islam is that the "way of submission" involves faithfully practicing Five Pillars:

1. *Recite the shahada.*
   The shahada is, "There is no god but Allah, and Mohammed is his prophet."

2. *Pray [salat] five times a day facing Mecca.*
   Faithful Muslims must pray each day at sunrise, noon, mid-afternoon, sunset and early evening.

3. *Give [zakat] alms to the poor.*
   Muslims are to give 2.5% of their income. Zakat includes giving from any plunder received by defeating an enemy.

4. *Fast [sawm] during the month of Ramadan.*
   The faithful must refrain from eating, drinking, smoking and sexual activity during the daylight hours of this holy month. Ramadan is the ninth month of the Muslim calendar, believed to be the month in which the Koran was originally revealed.

5. *Perform a pilgrimage [hajj] to Mecca at least once.*
   While in Mecca, certain sites must be visited and rituals performed. This Pillar may be waived if the participant cannot afford the trip.

Mohammed's Life

Mohammed's teaching caused strained relations in his home city of Mecca. In 622, when the leaders of his tribe turned against him, Mohammed and his followers relocated to the oasis of Yathrib, 250 miles north of Mecca. This famous journey is known as the "Hijra," or emigration. Yathrib was renamed "Medina" ("the City") and is the cradle of the Islamic faith. Mohammed conducted seven raids on merchant caravans traveling to Mecca over the next 18 months,[4] solidifying his position and power. In 624, he expelled the Jewish Quinuqa tribe from Medina and divided their properties among his followers. The following year, he did the same to the Nadir, a second Jewish tribe in the city. In the spring of 627, he charged the city's third Jewish tribe (the Quraiza) with collaboration with the enemy, beheaded the six to eight hundred men of the tribe and sold their women and children into slavery. Mohammed brought the surrounding Bedouin tribes under his influence and continued to increase in power until, in 630, Mecca capitulated to him.

On June 8, 632, the prophet died in the house of his favorite wife, A'isha. At the time of his death, Islamic power extended throughout most of the Arabian peninsula. Mohammed taught his followers, *"Believers, make war on the infidels who dwell around you. Deal firmly with them. Know that God is with the righteous."* (Sura 9:123) In a remarkable wave of victories over the next 100 years, Muslim troops conquered all of North Africa to the Atlantic, Spain, most of Asia Minor, Iraq, Iran and parts of India to the borders of China.[5]

View of the Afterlife: *Paradise*

Muslims believe that faithfully performing the Five Pillars of the faith will earn them entrance into Paradise. Paradise is a place of celebration and happiness. According to the Koran:

> *They shall recline on couches lined with thick brocade, and within reach will hang the fruits of both gardens. Which of the Lord's blessings would you deny? Therein are bashful virgins whom neither man nor jinnee will have touched before. Which of your Lord's blessings would you deny? Virgins as fair as coral and rubies..."* (Sura 55:54-60)

Another example:

> "*They shall recline on jeweled couches face to face, and there shall wait on them immortal youths with bowls and ewers and a cup of purest wine (that will neither pain their heads nor take away their reason); with fruits of their own choice and flesh of fowls that they will relish. And theirs shall be the dark-eyed houris, chaste as hidden pearls: a guerdon [reward] for their deeds.*" (Sura 56:15-25)

No mention is made of how women benefit from Paradise.

Islam in Comparison to Christianity

Islam and Christianity are both "evangelistic" religions. Mohammed commissioned his followers to bring the world into "Dar Islam" (the house of Islam). Christ commissioned His followers to "Go and make disciples of all nations." The methodology used in the advancement of these religions is strikingly different. Islam looks forward to a day when the whole world will recite, "There is no god but Allah and Mohammed is his Prophet,"[6] while Christianity looks for a day when "This gospel will be preached in the whole world as a testimony to all nations." (Matthew 24:14)

THINKING ABOUT IT

Something to Chew On:

Islam teaches that salvation is obtained through practicing the Five Pillars, hence earning a faithful Muslim a place in Paradise. Christianity teaches that salvation is a gift based on the efforts of Christ on our behalf.

Verse to Remember:

"Jesus said, 'You have heard it said, "Love your neighbor and hate your enemy." But I tell you: Love your enemies and pray for those who persecute you...'" Matthew 5:43-44

Point to Ponder:

What are the advantages of the Muslim view of life over the Christian view? What are the advantages of the Christian life?

My Thoughts on the Subject:

WHAT DO HINDUS BELIEVE?

"Just as man is destined to die once, and after that to face judgment, so Christ was sacrificed once to take away the sins of many people; and he will appear a second time, not to bear sin, but to bring salvation to those who are waiting for him."

Hebrews 9:27

Hinduism teaches an eternity of lifetimes followed by "Nivana," which is a cosmic nothingness. Hinduism has roughly 900 million followers today. The word *Hindu* is Persian for "Indian." 70% of the nation of India follows the Hindu religion.

View of God: *Pantheism*

Hinduism has roughly 900 million followers today. According to Hindu belief, **Brahman** is the universal spirit, which is everywhere and in everything. It is the unconscious, impersonal force that governs the whole universe. So Hinduism is a **pantheistic** religion. ("Pan" is the Latin word for "all.") Hindus believe that God is in everything. Brahman is the great force, the **circle of life** that ordains everything and puts everything in its place.

Over the centuries, Hindu holy men have written down their thoughts on how to get along in this world and the next. Hindus hold these writings as sacred. The main Hindu holy books are *The Vedas* (there are four of them) and *The Upanishads* (a series of elaborations on The Vedas).

Central Teaching: *Reincarnation*

Hinduism dates back to 3000 B.C. As ancient Hindus looked around their landscape, they noticed a certain hierarchy to our world. The fish eats the worm, the cat eats the fish, the coyote eats the cat, the mountain lion eats the coyote, the mountain lion gets captured by the game warden and transported to a safer place so that he won't eat the game warden's children. They also noted that even this

"Just as the body casts off worn out clothes and puts on new ones, so the infinite, immortal self casts off worn out bodies and enters into new ones." Krishna, The Bhagavad-Gita 2:22

hierarchy tends to go through a predictable cycle: The game warden dies, is buried in the ground, worms eat his body and the whole thing begins over again. From this, Hindu peoples developed their concept of the road to heaven called **"the transmigration of souls,"** or reincarnation. They believe that all life has an animating force that inhabits certain physical forms based on its level of goodness, as earned in previous lives.

Here's an example from one of Hinduism's sacred writings:

> *The murderer of a Brahmin becomes consumptive, the killer of a cow becomes hump-backed and imbecile, the murderer of a virgin becomes leprous — all three born as outcasts. The slayer of a woman and the destroyer of embryos becomes a savage full of diseases; who commits illicit intercourse, a eunuch; who goes with his teacher's wife, disease-skinned.*

The eater of flesh becomes very red; the drinker of intoxicants, one with discolored teeth.... Who steals food becomes a rat; who steals grain becomes a locust... perfumes, a muskrat; honey, a gadfly; flesh, a vulture; and salt, an ant.... Who commits unnatural vice becomes a village pig; who consorts with a Sudra woman becomes a bull; who is passionate becomes a lustful horse.... These and other signs and births are seen to be the karma of the embodied, made by themselves in this world. Thus the makers of bad karma, having experienced the tortures of hell, are reborn with the residues of their sins, in these stated forms (Garuda Purana 5).

In the 20th century, Indian gurus began emigrating to the United States and presenting their teachings on reincarnation. Upwardly mobile, optimistic Americans didn't like the idea that we could regress in our development. The American dream is about more, never less. So when Hinduism came to America, we modified the transmigrational highway, making it run only one way—up. This belief system has become known as "The New Age Movement." The New Age Movement believes in reincarnation, but never in a downward direction. New Age teachers proclaim that we are all gods, and that the god-part of us can't go backwards, only forwards. This belief in purely upward mobility is called "Cosmic Optimism."

The goal of Hindus is to live a life that merits good karma, which will enable them to progress forward on the transmigrational highway in their next life here on earth. If they do this well enough, over time they will advance to the highest level of humanity, which is the caste of Hindu priest called "Brahman." If a Brahman stores up enough karma, eventually he will be elevated out of physical existence into a state of semi-godhood, and he'll become a spirit. If he does very well in that spirit life, he'll be able to advance to the next higher spirit life.

View of the Afterlife: *Nirvana*

The ultimate goal of a Hindu is to become pure spirit, completely one with the Brahman of the universe. Achieving this state is called "Nirvana," which literally means "blown away." Because the Hindus' god is an impersonal force that inhabits all things, when people achieve Nirvana they lose all sense of consciousness and become absorbed into the unconsciousness of the universe. So the pathway to Nirvana involves multiple lifetimes of living well, dying well and being born again. Hindu scholars estimate that it takes roughly 600,000 lifetimes to achieve Nirvana.

Hinduism in Comparison to Christianity

The Bible mentions only eight people coming back from the dead. The prophets Elijah (1 Kings 17:17-24) and Elisha (2 Kings 4:31-36) each raised one, as did the Apostles Peter (Acts 9:37-40) and Paul (Acts 20:10). Three more were raised by Jesus[7], and the eighth was Jesus Christ Himself. The Bible teaches that everyone else has only one earthly life, as explained in Hebrews 9:27: *"Just as people are destined to die once, and after that to face judgment, so Christ was sacrificed once to take away the sins of many; and he will appear a second time, not to bear sin, but to bring salvation to those who are waiting for him."*

THINKING ABOUT IT

Something to Chew On:

Hinduism teaches an eternity of lifetimes followed by cosmic unity with an impersonal spirit. Christianity teaches one lifetime followed by eternity with a God who knows us personally.

Verse to Remember:

"... *people are destined to die once, and after that to face judgment...*" Hebrews 9:27

Point to Ponder:

What are the advantages of the Hindu view of life over the Christian view? What are the advantages of the Christian life over Hinduism?

My Thoughts on the Subject:

WHAT DO BUDDHISTS BELIEVE?

"Therefore, since Christ suffered in his body, arm yourselves also with the same attitude, because he who has suffered in his body is done with sin. And as a result, he does not live the rest of his earthly life for evil human desires, but rather for the will of God."

1 Peter 4:1-2

Buddhism has roughly 376 million adherents, which equates to about 6% of the world's population. Its founder, Siddhartha Gautama, was born in approximately 563 B.C. to a high caste Hindu family in Nepal. At about the age of 40, Gautama concluded that Hinduism was an inadequate system of belief. So he meditated under a fig tree for 40 days and nights to consider the matter. During this meditation, he became "enlightened" about the nature of life and the means to eternity. For the next 50 years, he was known as "The Buddha," which means "The Enlightened One."

View of God: *"A Noble Silence"*

According to Buddhism, God is beyond description. A leading Buddhist scholar claims:

"The Buddhist teaching on God, in the sense of an ultimate Reality, is neither agnostic, as is sometimes

claimed, nor vague, but clear and logical. Whatever Reality may be, it is beyond the conception of the finite intellect; it follows that attempts at description are misleading, unprofitable, and a waste of time. For these good reasons, the Buddha maintained about Reality, 'a noble silence.'"[8]

Central Teachings: *The Four Noble Truths* and *The Eightfold Path*

During his meditation, the Buddha discovered The Four Noble Truths. These truths explain the reality of life.

1. *Suffering is universal.* The very act of living brings about pain and suffering. If you are human, you will suffer.

2. *Craving is the root cause of suffering.* If we didn't desire things, we wouldn't feel deprived or lacking or that our lives weren't exactly what we want them to be.

3. *The cure for suffering is to eliminate craving.*

4. *Craving is eliminated by following The Eightfold Path.*

The Eightfold Path involves the following:

1. *Right views* (right understanding of The Four Noble Truths)

2. *Right thought* (about truth)

3. *Right speech* (no lying, no slander, no cruel words)

4. *Right behavior* (no killing any living creatures, no stealing, no sexual misconduct)

5. *Right occupation* (seek gainful employment)

6. *Right effort* (to attain enlightenment, strive to rid yourself of all your bad qualities, seek human perfection)

7. *Right contemplation* (be alert and observant of all that's going on around you in this life)

8. *Right meditation* (to enter enlightenment)

The ultimate goal of Buddhism is to be free from pain and suffering. By following his Eightfold Path, The Buddha taught that a person could achieve "enlightenment." Buddhism teaches, *"Those who love a hundred have a hundred woes. Those who love ten have ten woes. Those who love one have one woe. Those who love none have no woes."*[9] So Buddhism does not focus so much on the afterlife but on this life and the way to overcome suffering, which is to detach yourself from it.

> *"Man is born alone, lives alone and dies alone, and it is he alone who can blaze the way which leads him to Nirvana."* The Buddha

View of the Afterlife: *Nirvana*

Like the Hinduism from which it sprang, Buddhism believes in Nirvana but with a slight twist. Because Buddha saw all life and life forms as temporary, there is no "ultimate place."

> *Traditional [Buddhist] teaching is that there are six realms of existence into which one can be reborn: as a hell being, a "hungry" ghost, an animal, a human being, a jealous god and a heavenly being. The most precious of these is seen to be the human birth as this gives the best opportunities for winning enlightenment. A heavenly being is too absorbed in pleasure to think about winning enlightenment. Unlike Christianity, Buddhism sees these states as ultimately temporary. A god, therefore, will eventually descend into one of the lower realms.*[10]

For a Buddhist, the ultimate destination of the soul is fluid; it changes from one life to the next. The path to enlightenment is through disengagement from the cares of this world. If God exists, he or it is an impersonal force best not discussed since we cannot adequately describe Him.

Buddhism in Comparison to Christianity

Christianity takes a far different view of suffering and detachment. It says that suffering is profitable in many ways. According to the Bible, Jesus Christ, God's Son, didn't avoid suffering; He deliberately chose it on behalf of mankind. Jesus told His followers in Luke 9:22, *"The Son of Man must suffer many things and be rejected by the elders... and he must be killed, and on the third day be raised to life."*

Hebrews 2:18 says, *"Because he himself suffered when he was tempted, he is able to help those who are being tempted."* In Hebrews 4:15, it says that because Jesus suffered, He is able to *"sympathize with our weaknesses."* Furthermore, Hebrews 5:8 says that Christ *"learned obedience from what he suffered."*

Hebrews 4:17 teaches Christ's followers to *"Endure hardship as discipline,"* because going through hardship builds character. Romans 5:3-4 explains that *"...suffering produces perseverance; perseverance, character; and character, hope."* Elsewhere, 2 Corinthians 2:4 explains that suffering enables Christ-followers to *"...comfort those in any trouble with the comfort we ourselves have received from God."*

The Apostle Paul in 2 Timothy 2:3 goes so far as to encourage his friends to *"Endure hardship with us like a good soldier of Christ Jesus,"* and in 2 Timothy 1:8 to *"join with me in suffering for the gospel,"* so that others will be able to hear and understand God's message of love for them.

In this way, Christianity is the antithesis of Buddhism. Christ entered into the sufferings of the world in order to help the world. He taught His disciples to do the same. Buddha attempted to detach himself from his sufferings and the sufferings of the world, and he taught his disciples to do likewise. As 20th-century mathematician and philosopher Alfred North Whitehead said, *"Buddha gave his doctrine; Christ gave his life."*

THINKING ABOUT IT

Something to Chew On:

Buddhism teaches that the Eightfold Path is the path to the good life. Christianity teaches that following Christ is the path to the good life.

Verse to Remember:

"Because he himself suffered when he was tempted, he is able to help those who are being tempted." Hebrews 2:18

Point to Ponder:

What are the advantages of the Buddhist view of life over the Christian view? What are the advantages of the Christian view? Which system seems more believable, and why?

My Thoughts on the Subject:

WHAT DO CHRISTIANS BELIEVE?

"For it is by grace you have been saved, through faith—and this not from yourselves, it is the gift of God—not by works, so that no one can boast."

Ephesians 2:8-9

Christianity's founder, Jesus Christ, was born in Bethlehem, probably around 4 B.C. At age 30, Jesus began to heal, teach and perform miracles while preparing His disciples to carry on His ministry. In April of 29 A.D., He was crucified, buried and resurrected from the grave[11]. For 40 days He appeared to people before finally ascending into Heaven[12].

Ten days later, the Holy Spirit descended on Jesus' followers, empowering them to preach, heal and perform miracles[13]. The Christian church was born. Today Christianity is the largest religion or organization on earth, with some two billion followers worldwide. It is estimated that as many as 100,000 people become Christians each day.[14]

View of God: *Monotheism*

Christianity teaches that God is One Person manifesting Himself in three personalities (Father, Son and Holy Spirit). This is illustrated in Genesis 1, where God the Father *speaks* creation into existence while the Spirit is present. "Speaks" is a reference to the second person of the Trinity, called "the Word" in John 1:1. Father, Son and Holy Spirit were all present at the creation as documented in Genesis 1:26. He's a God in community with Himself. This is confirmed at the end of Genesis 1 where, instead

> "There are many religions in the world but only one Christianity, for only Christianity has a God who gave Himself for mankind. World religions attempt to reach up to God; Christianity is God reaching down to man." Billy Graham

of saying "I am going to make people in *my* image," He says, "Let *us* make people in *our* image." Thus God, who is in community, wanted to extend that community, so He created people like Himself. One of Christianity's central teachings is that men and women were created to have a relationship with God.

Central Teaching: *Grace*

The Bible says, *"It is not good for a man to be alone."*[15] The dilemma of mankind is that because of our separation from God, we feel alone. Every culture in every age has had a belief in God and a desire to be united with Him in some way. Christianity's solution to God and men getting together is an amazing thing called *grace*.

The Bible also says, *"Without the shedding of blood, there is no forgiveness of sins."*[16] In the Bible, blood is shed to pay for sins. Presumed in this is the concept of justice. Justice demands payment when a wrong has occurred. All of us want justice; we don't want to live in a world where God treats Saddam Hussein and Mother Teresa alike. We want things to be fair.

God wants justice, too. But, because He is also loving, He wants to give more than justice; He wants to give mercy. How can He be merciful while maintaining justice? By demanding payment, then paying it Himself. That's grace. The Bible describes it this way: *"When the kindness and love of God our Savior appeared, he saved us, not because of the righteous things we had done, but because of his mercy."*[17]

Four Solutions

In Genesis 3, Adam and Eve ate the forbidden fruit, and their sin caused separation from God. For the next eight chapters, God did something very creative: before He gave the **grace solution**, He demonstrated the futility of the solutions that each of the other three major religions will eventually devise.

The Isolation Solution

In Genesis 4, God demonstrated the **isolation solution**. Cain and Abel gave offerings to God. Cain's was a half-hearted offering, and God said in effect, "You can do better than that." In his frustration, Cain lashed out and killed his brother. God said, "Cain, from now on, you are going to live in isolation from the rest of the community." He banished Cain from the rest of humanity so that he wouldn't hurt or be hurt by them.

This is the Buddhist solution: Withdraw yourself. If you can't be touched, then you can't be hurt. This solution didn't work for Cain. He cried out, "My punishment is too great for me to bear!"[18]

The Repetition Solution

God demonstrated the second solution, the **repetition solution**, in Genesis 6. People were doing things to each other that were so hurtful, God caused a giant flood to eliminate all mankind, except the family of Noah. He then started humanity over again with this one ideal family.

This is the solution of Hinduism and the New Age Movement. With enough reincarnations, eventually you will achieve enough good karma to get close to God. The problem? No matter how many chances we get, we're still flawed and finite people, so we continue to make mistakes. This solution didn't work for Noah either; as soon as Noah's children stepped out of the boat, they got into a family feud. Noah got drunk, one of his sons ridiculed him, and Noah cursed the son and all his descendants.[19]

The Exertion Solution

In Genesis 11, on the plains of Babylon, people got together and tried to work their way back to God. They built a tower stretching toward the sky; their plan was to work hard enough to earn their way to heaven. The **exertion solution** is by far the most common response to the problem of aloneness. Islam says, "Work the Five Pillars. Given enough effort, you'll earn your way to Paradise." The Mormons, Jehovah's Witnesses and dozens of other minor religions have all adopted strategies for earning their way to God.

The Relation Solution

After God got through demonstrating the inadequacies of these methods, He began to put His own solution into place. His solution is a relationship based on grace. In Genesis 12, God chose one man, Abraham. He built a relationship with him and began to teach him about grace. He promised that He would turn Abraham into a great nation that would bless "all peoples on earth." [20]

In Exodus 12, God introduced the nation of Israel to the idea of simultaneously fulfilling justice and giving mercy by providing a substitute payment for the people's sins. God said to Moses, *"Tell the whole community of Israel that on the tenth day of this month each man is to take a lamb for his family.... The animals you choose must be year-old males without defect.... Take care of them until the fourteenth day of the month, when all the people of the community of Israel must slaughter them at twilight."*[21] The lamb served as the grace solution for the people. The forfeit of its life served as payment for sin, allowing God to maintain justice while giving grace.

This idea reached its fulfillment in Jesus Christ. On the day Christ began His ministry, John the Baptist declared, *"Behold! The Lamb of God who takes away the sin of the world!"*[22] For the next three and a half years, Jesus proclaimed that the kingdom of God was at hand. At the end of that time, He was led up a hill to his death, like an innocent lamb to the slaughter. After several hours on the cross, Jesus looked up to heaven and said, *"It is finished."*[23] This was God's solution to man's separation from Him: He enforced justice by taking a life, but the life He took was the life of His Son. God grants forgiveness based on the merits of another.

The Bible says, *"To all who believed him and accept him, he gave the right to become children of God."*[24] In Christianity, instead of asking us to make the effort, God makes the effort for us.

So every person in the world is only one prayer away from heaven. The prayer is a simple request: *"Lord, thank You for what Christ did for me on the Cross. Please accept His sin payment on my behalf and be my Lord."*

View of the Afterlife: *Heaven*

The Bible describes heaven as a place in God's presence, where there will be no more tears, death, mourning or pain (Revelation 21). Entrance is granted based on knowing Christ. People from every culture and language will be there (Revelation 7). And everyone will be given responsibilities commensurate with those they assumed for Christ here on earth.[25]

THINKING ABOUT IT

Something to Chew On:

Christianity is unique. Instead of asking us to make the effort, God makes the effort for us.

Verse to Remember:

"For it is by God's grace that you have been saved through faith. It is not the result of your own efforts, but God's gift, so that no one can boast about it." Ephesians 2:8-9, TEV

Point to Ponder:

If I were God and wanted a relationship with mankind, what would I do to demonstrate my love for people?

My Thoughts on the Subject:

WHAT DO THE OTHER RELIGIONS BELIEVE?

"Jesus answered, 'I am the way, the truth and the life. No one can come to the Father except through me.' "

John 14:6 NLT

In recent years, sociologists have studied and catalogued every religious system that has 10,000 or more followers. The following chart displays the largest of these religions, along with each one's percentage of followers.[26]

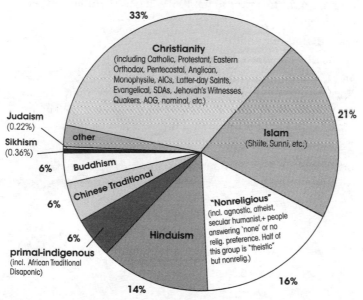

33%

Christianity
(including Catholic, Protestant, Eastern Orthodox, Pentecostal, Anglican, Monophysite, AICs, Latter-day Saints, Evangelical, SDAs, Jehovah's Witnesses, Quakers, AOG, nominal, etc.)

21%

Islam
(Shiite, Sunni, etc.)

Judaism
(0.22%)

Sikhism
(0.36%)

other

6% **Buddhism**

6% **Chinese Traditional**

6% **primal-indigenous**
(incl. African Traditional Disaponic)

Hinduism

"Nonreligious"
(incl. agnostic, atheist, secular humanist,+ people answering 'none' or no relig. preference. Half of this group is "theistic" but nonrelig.)

16%

14%

NOTE: Total adds up to more than 100% due to rounding and because upper bound estimates were used for each group.

©2005 www.adherents.com

117

You may be surprised to learn that there are very few truly viable religions; 97% of the world adheres to one of only seven religions. Increase this number to the top 10 religions, and you'll include 98% of humanity.

What about the other hundreds of religions practiced around the world? Their adherence numbers are so small that if any one of them is right, then more than 99.8% of us are wrong. Admittedly, perhaps *all* religions are wrong, but if there is one right religion, surely we will find it among the top 10. Let's explore them from smallest to largest:

#10—JUCHE

FOLLOWERS = 19 million North Koreans (.03%)	
FOUNDER = Kim Il Sung, 1950s	

Juche is the national religion of North Korea, also known as "kimilsungism." It was created and mandated by Kim Il Sung, North Korea's first communist dictator, soon after he came to power in the 1950s. It has 19 million adherents because North Korea has 19 million inhabitants, and it is the only government-authorized ideology of the state. "Juche" means "self-reliance" in Korean, and its promoters describe it as a secular, ethical philosophy and not a religion. But from a sociological viewpoint, Juche is a Korean blending of Marxist-Communist thought. It makes no claims about heaven and generates no belief that life after death even exists.

> *"All religions do not teach the same thing but differ at key points."* R.C. Sproul

#9—SIKHISM

FOLLOWERS = 23 million, chiefly in Punjab, India (.038%)	
FOUNDER = Guru Nanak, 1469	
VIEW OF GOD = Monotheism	
MEANS TO GOD = The Five "K's"	

The Sikh religion is a hybrid of Hinduism and Islam. Its founder was a man named Nanak who endured years of violence between the Muslims and the Hindus in his area. Nanak's solution to the problem of the war was to adopt the concept of monotheism from the Muslims and the concepts of karma and reincarnation from the Hindus. His revelation: *"There is no Hindu, there is no Muslim."* [27]

There are 23 million Sikhs, most of them living in the Indian state of Punjab, though some of them have emigrated to the U.K., Canada, the U.S., Malaysia and Singapore. The Sikhs are monotheists. In order to escape the endless wandering of the soul that happens as reincarnation follows reincarnation, a devout Sikh must carry certain articles of faith at all times. They are known as "The Five K's" and are worn to identify and represent Sikhism ideals:

1. *Kesh: "uncut hair" for honesty*
2. *Kanga: "wooden comb" for equality*
3. *Kaccha: "specially designed underwear" for fidelity*
4. *Kara: "metal bracelet" for meditation*
5. *Kirpan: "strapped sword" for never bowing to tyranny*

Interestingly, Sikhs make up 10-15% of the Indian army and 20% of its officers, which makes them 10 times more likely to be a soldier and officer in the Indian army than the average Indian. Because of the turbans they customarily wear, many Westerners mistake Sikhs for Muslims or even terrorists, which has resulted in a recent increase of hate crimes against Sikhs in the U.S. and Britain since the events of 9/11.

#8—African Traditional Religion

FOLLOWERS = 95 million in Africa and places where Africans were enslaved (1.6%)	
VIEW OF GOD = Polytheism	
MEANS TO GOD = Sacrifices	

This religion is actually a large grouping of religions. Among its various tribes and adaptations, there are approximately 95 million people who practice this form of animism. *Animism* is the spiritual belief that all creation (plants and animals, rocks and rivers, sand and soil) possesses *animation* or life within them. African traditional religion's view of God is that many gods inhabit every rock and tree, the sky, the moon and the sun.

Animistic religions believe that the means to gain favor with the gods is to make sacrifices to them, and pleasing the gods is the key to reaching the afterlife. Many ancient animistic cultures practiced human sacrifice, including the Druids of Northern Europe; the Mayans, Aztecs and Incas of Latin America; and most of the peoples of the ancient Near East. Modern animists tend to use animals and sometimes flowers or plants as offerings.

Animists believe in a heaven that is not too different than life on earth. For example, old American westerns used to feature Native Americans talking about "The Happy Hunting Grounds," a spirit-world after death where life is similar to, but better than, present human life. The movie *Gladiator* pictures General Maximus Meridius walking through the "Elysian Fields," after his death. The ancient Greek and Roman pagans believed in this type of afterlife existence.

#7—Primal-Indigenous

FOLLOWERS = 150 million, including shamans (Siberia), pagans (in Asia and India) and smaller, pre-literate tribal belief systems (2.5%)	

This group of religions is comprised of animists who still live on the fringes of literate society. Primal-Indigenous peoples' beliefs are similar to African Traditional Religionists, so they used to be all grouped together as simply "animists." But demographers have separated the two groups in recent years out of respect for their distinctive ethnicities.

#6—Chinese Traditional Religions	
FOLLOWERS =	225 million, mostly in China (4%)
FOUNDERS =	Lao-Tse (604-531 B.C.) and Confucius (551-479 B.C.)
VIEW OF GOD =	No particular deity/impersonal force (though Lao-Tse did become venerated generations later)
MEANS TO GOD =	Not stressed; more of an ethical system than a religious one

As the name implies, most of Chinese Traditional Religionists live in China. Lao-Tse founded Taoism, and Confucius founded Confucianism. Both are chiefly concerned with how to live an honorable life by treating people well and venerating one's ancestors. None of the major branches of this group concern themselves much with God or the afterlife. Chinese Traditional Religions have more of a here-and-now focus.

#5—Buddhism	
FOLLOWERS =	360 million (6%)
FOUNDER =	Siddhartha Guatama (563-483 B.C.)
VIEW OF GOD =	Not stressed
MEANS TO GOD =	The Four Noble Truths

Like Chinese Traditional Religions, Buddha focused on how to live here and now. As we discussed earlier, most branches of Buddhism do not stress or describe God or an afterlife.

#4—Secularism/Nonreligious/Agnostics/Atheists

FOLLOWERS =	850 million, nonreligious Westerns, agnostics and atheists in current and former communist countries (14%)

Scholars lump these groups together because they all purport a lack of interest in religion or spirituality. But one observer notes, "Sociologists point out that there are no truly 'secular' societies... 'nonreligious' people... are those who derive their worldview and value system from alternative, secular, cultural or otherwise nonrevealed systems rather than traditional religious systems."[28] Some, like Michael Newdow who was mentioned on Day 6, would say, "I don't really know what I believe. And it doesn't really matter." Many have made the conscious choice not to explore their faith, or at least not publicly.

#3—Hinduism

FOLLOWERS =	900 million (15%)
FOUNDED =	1800-1000 B.C.
VIEW OF GOD =	Pantheism, Universal life force
MEANS TO GOD =	Transmigrational highway
VIEW OF AFTERLIFE =	Nirvana

#2—Islam	
FOLLOWERS = 1.3 billion (22%)	
FOUNDER = Mohammed, 610 A.D.	
VIEW OF GOD = Monotheism	
MEANS TO GOD = The Five Pillars of Islam	
VIEW OF AFTERLIFE = Paradise	

#1—Christianity	
FOLLOWERS = 2 billion (33%)	
FOUNDER = Jesus Christ, 33 A.D.	
VIEW OF GOD = Monotheism (Trinitarian)	
MEANS TO GOD = Atonement/Substitution	
VIEW OF AFTERLIFE = Heaven	

Some Observations

Every religion claims to be the only way to God. Every religion has a different road, and almost all the roads seem to lead to different places. To help you make a choice between them, try answering these questions: *Which of these systems matches the description of how life seems to work on earth? Which of them offers the most believable description of God? Which of them matches what your heart tells you is true?*

THINKING ABOUT IT

Something to Chew On:

The world's 10 largest religions offer a diversity of choices of belief, but very few points in common. While all of them may be wrong, only one of them can be right.

Verse to Remember:

"Serve the Lord. But if serving the Lord seems undesirable to you, then choose for yourselves this day whom you will serve..." Joshua 24:14-15

Point to Ponder:

Of all the choices presented today, which do I believe is most likely to lead me to God?

My Thoughts on the Subject:

Sabbath

A Day of Rest

If you ever find yourself in the city of Jerusalem over a weekend, you'll discover something interesting about Sabbaths. Muslim shops are closed on Fridays, Jewish shops on Saturdays, and Christian shops on Sunday.

Observant Muslims gather at the Mosque at noon on Fridays, where they hear a sermon, followed by a time of prayer. They call this service "Jumu'ah." The Hebrew meaning of "Sabbath" is "seventh." Jews take the seventh day off because that's the day on which God rested from His work of creation. Most Christians take the first day of the week off, because that's the day Christ rose from the dead:

"On the first day of the week, very early in the morning, the women took the spices they had prepared and went to the tomb. They found the stone rolled away from the tomb, but when they entered, they did not find the body of the Lord Jesus." (Luke 24:1-3)

"On the first day of the week, we came together to break bread." (Acts 20:7)

Go to church today, and start Week Four tomorrow.

END NOTES

ISN'T "ONLY ONE WAY" TOO NARROW?

1. Symmachus was Prefect of Rome in 384, when Emperor Valentinian II commanded that the pagan Altar of Victory be removed from the Roman Senate. This is Symmachus' reasoning for letting it remain. Reference: *Medieval Sourcebook: Ambrose: Dispute with Symmachus*, found at http://www.fordham.edu/halsall/source/ambrose-sym.html (Also: *Nicene and Post-Nicene Fathers*, second series, vol. 10, New York, 1896) p. 414.

2. Adapted from R.C. Sproul, *Reason to Believe* (Grand Rapids: Zondervan, 1982) p. 41-43.

WHAT DO MUSLIMS BELIEVE?

3. According to Phil Parshall (*New Paths in Muslim Evangelism: Evangelical Approaches to Contextualization* [Grand Rapids: Baker, 1980] p. 142), *"Muslims generally believe the dynamic of the Trinity consists of God the Father's having sexual intercourse with Mary the mother of Jesus, who was the second member of the Trinity. This union resulted in the birth of Jesus as the third person of the Godhead."*

4. Karsh, Efraim, *Islamic Imperialism*, London: Yale University Press, 2007, p. 14.

5. Langer, William, editor, *The Encyclopedia of World History, Sixth Edition*, New York: Houghton Mifflin, 2001, pp. 108-109.

6. Karsh, Islamic Imperialism, p. 1.

WHAT DO HINDUS BELIEVE?

7. The son of the widow of Nain (Luke 7:11-16), the daughter of Jairus (Mark 5:35-42), and Jesus' friend Lazarus (John 11:14-44).

WHAT DO BUDDHISTS BELIEVE?

8. Quoted in Colin Chapman, *Christianity on Trial* (Herts, England: Lion, 1974) p. 226.

9. Steve Kumar, *Christianity for Skeptics* (Peabody, MA.: Hurt Publishing, 2000) p. 129.

10. Anthony Flanagan, "Rebirth" (located at http://buddhism.about.com/library/weekly/aa071602a.htm).

WHAT DO CHRISTIANS BELIEVE?

11. 1 Corinthians 15:3.
12. Acts 1:9.
13. Acts 2:1.
14. Source: David Barrett and Todd Johnson's annual report, available at http://www.jesus.org.uk/dawn/2003/dawn16.html and http://gem-werc.org/.
15. Genesis 2:18.
16. Hebrews 9:22.
17. Titus 3:5-6.
18. Genesis 4:13.
19. Genesis 9:21-25.
20. Genesis 12:3.
21. Exodus 12:3-6.
22. John 1:29.
23. John 19:30.
24. John 1:12.
25. Matthew 25:23.

WHAT DO THE OTHER RELIGIONS BELIEVE?

26. www.adherents.com. Note: Adherents.com is a sociological site that analyzes religious groups and trends. The authors of this book do not classify Latter-Day Saints and Jehovah's Witnesses as part of the Christian movement.

27. Guru Nanak, circa 1469.

28. www.adherents.com/Religion_by_Adherents.html.

MAJOR QUESTION:

How Can a Good God Allow Suffering?

"Yet when I hoped for good, evil came; when I looked for light, then came darkness. The churning inside me never stops; days of suffering confront me."

Job 30.20-27

"It is a problem which no theist will avoid and no honest thinker will try to avoid."

Elton Trueblood

WHAT ARE
THE POSSIBILITIES?

"Why are you holding onto your integrity?
Curse God and die!"

Job 2:9

We gave the members of our church an assignment: Ask your neighbors, "If you could ask God any question, what would you like to know?" The *"Why is there suffering?"* question won hands down. *"If God is all-knowing, then He is aware of everything that goes on. If He is all-powerful, then He can prevent or correct anything bad. And if He is completely loving, then He cares about everything that goes on. So, why is there suffering in the world?"*

Because the world contains so much sorrow and evil, many people conclude that God cannot be all-knowing, all-powerful and completely loving at the same time. He can be two out of three, but if He was all three, He could not possibly sit back and allow the tragedies that occur on our planet on a daily basis. Or could He? Today, we'll look at some of the ways different groups have answered the question of suffering.

A Two-Out-of-Three God

Maybe the reason suffering exists in the world is because God is all-knowing and all-powerful, but lacks love. If this is true, suffering exists because God doesn't care enough to do anything about it; He's at best disinterested, and at worst delighted, with the pain and hurt He sees inflicted on people and the planet. A second possibility is that God is all-powerful and all-

"Pain is weakness leaving the body." U.S. Marines T-shirt

loving, but lacks the ability to know and see everything that is going on, so evil and suffering often slip by Him. The third possibility is that God is all-loving and all-knowing, but lacks power; He simply can't prevent evil from happening.

Option #1 leaves us with a scary God, a God who knows about everything and is strong enough to do anything. He is unrestrained; no compassion or morals keep Him from torturing His creation. He can change the rules, both moral and physical, any time He wishes. Tomorrow morning we might wake up to find that gravity no longer holds, or that photosynthesis doesn't work, or that justice is now not a virtue but a vice.

Option #2 gives us a blind God. This God is strong and loving, but slow because He can't foresee, or even see, what is presently going on with us. This God wants to help; it just takes Him a while. Option #3 brings us a weak God. He sees everything and wants to help; He just can't, because He's not strong enough.

All three of these options are flawed. God #1 makes no sense. None of us goes to bed worried that the sun won't rise tomorrow or that water will suddenly begin running uphill. The universe appears to have a constancy and predictability to it.

God #2 is illogical. If the only reason evil keeps breaking out is because God can't see it coming or can't notice it taking place, why wouldn't this God, who created time, do a little rewinding and set it all right the second time around?

God #3 makes no sense either. This God is either an aging grandfather who once was able to do mighty things, or a custodial God who *was always* too weak to govern and control Nature. He's just sitting in for some-one stronger who, apparently, has left the scene.

Another Approach: Job and Friends

The book of Job was included in the Bible to help answer the question of suffering. Scholars believe Job may have been written as an ancient drama to be acted out on the stage. Those with major speaking parts are Job, his wife, his friends and God. Once Job poses the question, "Why is this happening to me?" the remaining characters give answers according to their own understanding.

Answer One: Who's to Blame?

Job's wife gives the first answer. When Job finds that his wealth, health and children have all been taken from him, she suggests that Job put an end to his misery by putting an end to his life. Her exact words are, "Curse God and die!"

Bitterness and blame are often the reactions of people in or near suffering. In the face of such seeming unfairness, many would go so far as to conclude God doesn't even exist. Funny thing, though: most people who conclude that there isn't a God at all still blame the God *who isn't out there* for the problems in the universe. They've stopped believing, but they haven't stopped blaming.

If God doesn't exist, then where did we ever get the notion that life should be fair in the first place? Where did that sense of justice come from?

Answer Two: So It's My Fault

Job's friends give a second answer. As Eliphaz, Bildad and Zophar sit down with Job and watch him pick scabs, they listen and lament with him. But after listening to Job for a few days, they've had enough and start giving advice. They say things like, *"Consider now, who, being innocent, has ever perished?"*[1] And *"All his days the wicked man suffers torment..."*[2] And *"The mirth of the wicked is brief, the joy of the godless lasts a moment."*[3] For all their initial compassion, these friends are now saying, "Face it, Job, you sinned. That's why you're suffering." It's the moralist answer to evil: The world has a balance to it, and you only get what you deserve.

Answer Three: God's Perspective

After listening to everyone's platitudes for almost 40 chapters, God brings His own answer to the question. When He does, He rebukes Job's friends for their lack of compassion: "What you're saying is the wrong message, given at the wrong time in the wrong way." When people are in pain, God never responds with a platitude. (At the end of the book of Job, God even tells these friends, "You owe Job an apology.") From Chapters 38 to 41, God answers Job in a way that puts the question into perspective — *God's* perspective.

Only when we see the problem of pain from the perspective of God can we hope to find a true, whole, sense-making answer. Toward the close of the book, as Job raises his voice and demands an explanation from God, God answers him, "Job, where were you when I hung the constellations? Can you explain where light comes from? Or how darkness came into being? Can you understand the miracle of how conception takes place?"

God's answer to Job when he asks "why" is not about suffering; it's about Job himself. God reminds Job of who is God and who is not. It's not a very satisfying answer to me, but it is to Job. After God speaks, Job says, *"Surely I spoke of things I did not understand, things too wonderful for me to know... Therefore I despise myself and repent in dust and ashes."* [4]

But I Want an Explanation!

I have thought about this for a while, and it occurs to me that when calamity strikes someone I love, I want an explanation. But when calamity strikes me, I want comfort. But God explains to Job that He doesn't owe Job an explanation. He doesn't really owe you or me one, either. Besides, if He really is God, 99.9% of the explanation would be over our heads anyway. Frederick Buechner says, "For God to try to explain the kinds of things Job wants explained would be like Einstein explaining relativity to a littleneck clam." I like the way author Philip Yancey puts it: "Maybe sometimes God keeps us in the dark about 'why' not so much because He wants to keep us in the dark, as because He knows we are incapable of absorbing so much light."

THINKING ABOUT IT

Something to Chew On

When someone I love is hurting, I want an explanation. When I am hurting, I want comfort.

Verse to Remember:

"My ears had heard of you but now my eyes have seen you. Therefore I despise myself and repent in dust and ashes." Job 42:5-6

Point to Ponder:

If I could ask God any one question, what would it be?

My Thoughts on the Subject:

DID GOD CREATE EVIL?

"...Sighing comes to me instead of food;
my groans pour out like water."

Job 3:24

The Bible says in John 16:33, *"In this world, you will have trouble."* My personal experience and the daily news broadcasts align with that description. This world is full of trouble.

How do you reconcile a troubled world with a good God? Shouldn't God do something about the trouble? The answer: He is doing something, but we may not be seeing the whole story.

If you have ever opened a novel and started reading at page 100, you know how confusing it can be. The Bible describes the beginning, middle and ending of history. Right now, we're in the middle of history. The whole thing makes much more sense if we can start at the beginning.

In the beginning, God created the heavens and the earth. The earth was a marvelous place; it was paradise. The pinnacle of God's earthly creation was the making of men and women. God made humans with high reasoning capacity and the ability to make choices for themselves. Another term for the ability to make choices is **free will**. To understand where suffering comes from, you have to understand free will.

The Option for Evil

In order to offer humankind real freedom, God created us with the ability to choose between right and wrong. In the midst of paradise, God designated one tree and said, *"You are free to eat from any tree in the garden; but you must not eat from the tree of the knowledge of good and evil."* [5]

Like a fish that has always lived in the ocean, Adam and Eve only knew one set of circumstances. A fish may live its whole life without experiencing air (which would be a good thing). But the day it jumps out of the water and takes air into its gills, it begins to understand what water really is.

Similarly, Adam and Eve had no need to know what evil was. But, in order to have free will, God gave them not only the option to choose between a number of good things, but also the option of choosing the evil thing. Evil wasn't God's choice for them (far from it), and He didn't create evil. But He did create the **potential for evil** by designating that one tree as "off-limits." Eventually, they chose to experience the "off-limits" option. Like the fish out of water, from that day forward, they knew what "good" was, because they had experienced its antithesis.

> *"You do not have to sit outside in the dark. If, however, you want to look at the stars, you will find that darkness is required. The stars neither require it nor demand it."* Annie Dillard

A Perfect World

Many people ask, *"Why didn't God create a world where there was no evil and suffering?"* Answer: He did.

The Bible's opening chapter describes God's creation, from land to plants to fish to birds to animals.

Every piece of creation was good. At the end of the full Creation, *"God saw all that he had made, and it was very good."*[6]

Evil and suffering are the result of the choice made by our first parents, Adam and Eve. *"When Adam sinned, sin entered the entire human race. Adam's sin brought death, so death spread to everyone, for everyone sinned."*[7]

Two Kinds of Evil

Human beings experience the effects of their sin, and Creation did as well. The Bible indicates that something damaging happened to the physical universe as a result of Adam and Eve's choice: *"...all creation has been groaning as in the pains of childbirth right up to the present time."*[8]

This explains natural phenomena that inflict harm on people. When Adam and Eve chose evil, they were telling God that they wanted some space. God honored that choice, and nature was cursed. Genetic breakdown and disease began. Pain and death became part of the human experience. Natural disasters like tornadoes, earthquakes, floods and famines sprang up.

While these "natural" types of calamity occur with regularity, someone has observed that about 95% of all suffering comes from what is called moral evil. Moral evil is evil inflicted on one person by another, or by a group of others. When someone dies from a tornado, that's **natural evil**; when they die from a stab wound, that's **moral evil**.

Why Would God Let This Happen?

Young couples often wrestle with the potential for birth defects and other dangers as they weigh the decision to have children. Most choose to go ahead in spite of the risks.

Why? Because of love, and because of a desire to have a relationship with someone in their own image. God made that same choice.

God created the potential for evil to enter the world because it was the only way He could create the potential for genuine goodness and genuine love. But it was human beings, in our free will, who brought that potential evil into reality.

THINKING ABOUT IT

Something to Chew On:

Love must be the most costly of all actions, because love will pay almost any price to be able to express itself.

Verse to Remember:

"God saw all that he had made, and it was very good."
Genesis 1:31

Point to Ponder

Faced with God's choice to create humans with the potential for evil or not to create them at all, what choice would I have made, and why?

My Thoughts on the Subject:

_____

_____

_____

_____

_____

_____

_____

WHAT'S THE POINT OF PROBLEMS?

"But he knows the way that I take; when he has tested me, I will come forth as gold."

Job 23:10

Nobody's immune to pain. In His famous Sermon on the Mount, Jesus said, *"[God] causes his sun to rise on the evil and the good, and sends rain on the righteous and the unrighteous..."* (Matthew 5:45) Nobody's immune to sunshine, and nobody's immune to rain.

This may not be great news, but it's not bad news either. It means that whatever hardship I am facing, I'm not the first one to experience it. God hasn't singled me out for cruel and unusual punishment. And if others have gotten through this kind of thing before, chances are I can, too. This helps me when I'm in trouble.

Every Problem Has a Purpose

However bad a situation may be, the pain of it is not senseless. Something good can come of my circumstances if I respond well to them. The Bible says that God uses problems in at least five redemptive ways in people's lives.

1. **God Uses Trials to *Direct* Me**
   Though donkeys have long been used as an animal for carrying and traveling, they can be

extremely stubborn at times. When they set their mind to keeping still, they will keep still until persuasive force is used. God knows that humans have something in common with the donkey: Sometimes we need to be hit over the head with a two-by-four to get us moving. The book of Proverbs says, "Sometimes it takes a painful situation to make us change our ways." [9] Problems often point us in a new direction and motivate us to change.

2. **God Uses Trials to *Inspect* Me**

   Someone once said, "People are like teabags; if you want to know what's inside them, just drop them into hot water!" The Bible says, "When you have many kinds of troubles, you should be full of joy, because you know that these troubles test your faith, and this will give you patience." [10]

3. **God Uses Trials to *Correct* Me**

   Some lessons can only be learned through pain or failure. Your parents probably told you not to touch a hot stove. But how did you learn not to touch a hot stove? By getting burned!

   Sometimes we only learn the value of something

   like health, money or a relationship by losing it. King David said about his pain, "It was the best thing that could have happened to me, for it taught me to pay attention to your laws." [11]

4. **God Uses Trials to *Protect* Me**

   A problem can be a blessing in disguise if it prevents you from being harmed by something more serious. For instance, I know of a man who lost his job for refusing to do something unethical at work. His unemployment was a trial, but it may have saved him from prison a year later when his employer's actions were uncovered.

5. **God Uses Trials to *Perfect* Me**

When we respond correctly to trials and troubles, they can become character-builders. "We can rejoice when we run into problems... they help us learn to be patient. And patience develops strength of character in us and helps us trust God more each time we use it until finally our hope and faith are strong and steady." [12]

The understanding of why I am experiencing pain doesn't generally come during the painful circumstance; I'm too numb or too close to the situation to see its lesson. Usually I discover the purpose behind my problem after it has been solved or endured. Still, knowing that my suffering can result in good (even if I can't instantly figure out what's good about it) lifts the burden a little bit. And I'm encouraged to think I live in a universe where everything, no matter how painful, can be used for good.

"God whispers to us in our pleasures, He speaks to us in our conscience, but He shouts to us in our pain. It is His megaphone to rouse a deaf world."

C.S. Lewis

Life is a series of problem-solving opportunities. My problems will either defeat me or develop me, depending on how I respond to them. So every problem has a piece of good news attached to it.

THINKING ABOUT IT

Something to Chew On:

1. Whatever I'm facing, I am not the only person to have gone through something like it.
2. Good can result from problems and suffering if I keep the right perspective.

Verse to Remember:

"We know that in all things God works for the good of those who love him..." Romans 8:28

Point to Ponder:

What might be the purpose behind the problem(s) I am currently facing?

My Thoughts on the Subject:

_____

_____

_____

_____

_____

_____

WHAT KIND OF ANSWER DO YOU NEED?

"I, even I, am he who comforts you."
Isaiah 51:12

"Why, God?" is by far the most commonly asked God Question. A young couple asked that question on the day they received the news that their two-month-old daughter had a congenital disease that would cause her much suffering and end her life early.

The little girl wasn't digesting her food well and wasn't growing as fast as others her age. During a routine check-up, her mother asked the doctor if something might be wrong. The unfortunate result of the test was summed up by the doctor: "Your daughter has cystic fibrosis."

The gene that causes this illness is recessive, so both parents must be carriers to pass it on. Neither the father nor mother knew of anyone in their family who had ever had the disease. Yet here it was. The little girl, Marcia, was my older sister.

Growing up, there was never a morning when Marcia didn't have to take a special pill to help her digest her food properly. By the time she was eight years old, her nightly routine included spending two hours with her head below her chest and my mom patting on her back to loosen the phlegm in her lungs.

By age 10, Marcia's condition had weakened her to the point where she spent at least two weeks a year in the hospital fighting pneumonia. At age 12, she was sleeping in an oxygen tent at night. When Marcia was 16, Dad moved out. I later learned that 85% of parents of children with cystic fibrosis divorce.

"God weeps with us so that we may one day laugh with Him." Jorgen Moltmann

The constant strain, pressure and financial drain are more than most marriages can endure. The most haunting memory of my young life came a year later when Marcia died. I heard the muffled sobs of my mother in her bedroom, grieving the loss of the child she had loved and cared for so dearly. Only one question was on my mind that night: "Why, God? Why?"

Two Kinds of Answers

I know my mother's pain. I watched it up close. But my father was more private about his suffering. Although he was raised in a religious home, his little girl's suffering raised questions beyond what his huge intellect could bear. Decades later, he remains unwilling to believe in a God who is all-knowing, all-powerful and all-loving, because he is unable to accept that such a God could sit back and do nothing while one of His children suffered so much.

When it comes to the question of suffering, there are two kinds of answers. One kind helps us understand— these are **logic-based answers**. A second kind helps us emotionally—these are **feeling-based answers**. Most people in pain have a hard time listening to logic. What they need first is something that touches their heart.

During the week I was writing this, a young man named Steve shared his story with our church. He arrived home one day to find the house empty, with a message that he was to join the family at the hospital. Upon entering the emergency room, he was greeted by the news that his father and brother had died in a traffic accident. A younger brother survived, but lost a third of his brain. In the 14 years since that accident, his brother endured 20 surgeries.

Steve loves God passionately. He serves on our vocal team, and his wife is part of our paid staff. But understandably, Steve has struggled deeply with trusting God after the loss of his father and brother. In moments of desperation, he has even considered taking his own life. His pain was and continues to be very real. But so is his faith. What has given Steve the resolve to continue to trust God? Two things: **compassion** and **community**.

During the dark night of his soul, members of his family and church wrapped their arms around him. He knew they cared. He experienced their compassion and community. More importantly, the answers Steve received spoke not only to his mind but to his **emotions**. Steve knows from experience the story of Christ's suffering on behalf of the sins of the world.

When we hurt, it is almost impossible to believe in a God who gave us enough free will to get ourselves into the mess we're in. While the answer of "free will" makes sense, it's not emotionally satisfying. When we hurt, we need to be touched emotionally, not just intellectually.

Steve knew that Christ had given the ultimate feeling-based answer to the problem of pain: He endured it Himself. When the question, "How could God put anyone through this much pain?" came to Steve, the answer was always, "This pain was not of God's doing, but He willingly suffered this level of pain, and more, for you." In the midst of his pain, Steve was touched by God's love—the deep love of a Father who not only says, "I am so sorry," but also says, "I know exactly how you feel."

When I hurt, I don't want logic, because I'm too numb to care that God is all-knowing and all-powerful. But I am touched by His love, a love that is so genuine it chose to suffer for me. I can respond to a God like that.

The answer that Steve needed was God's compassion. For most people who have been deeply wounded, knowing that there are intellectual answers, like the problem of free will, helps us a little. But experiencing His compassion through the love of Christ and the community of others heals us a lot.

I believe there were hints of God's compassion all over my sister's life and death. She was endowed with outstanding gifts and an astounding spirit. Everyone who knew her loved her. And, while I'm not sure about this, sometimes I wonder if the shortened span of her painful life was a gift from God. For the Bible says, *"No eye has seen, no ear has heard, no mind has conceived what God has prepared for those who love him."*[13] Rather than suffer in her diseased body for these last three decades, Marcia has been experiencing wonders I cannot yet begin to comprehend. I can believe in a God like that, because He demonstrated His compassion to me through His Son and the community of His church.

THINKING ABOUT IT

Something to Chew On:

Hurting people don't care how right an answer is until they experience how loving the answer feels.

Verse to Remember:

"Yet this I call to mind and therefore I hope: Because of the Lord's great love we are not consumed, for his compassions never fail. They are new every morning; great is your faithfulness." Lamentations 3:21-23

Point to Ponder:

How have I experienced the compassion and community of God? Does this help me trust Him? Why?

My Thoughts on the Subject:

WHICH ACT
ARE WE LIVING IN?

*"Never again will there be an infant who...
lives but a few days, or an old man who
does not live out his years..."*
Isaiah 65:20

We live in a moment in time. Because it's *our moment*, it feels like things will always be the way they are right now. But judging God and history based on our limited experience is shortsighted. Have you ever walked in on the middle of a movie? Suppose the television is on while you're walking through the living room. The scene on the screen is really engaging, so you stand there and watch for a few minutes. Inevitably, a dozen questions race through your mind: *Why did the hero do that? How did they get there? Who's this person over here?* Without a context, much of what you're watching makes no sense.

Right now, Planet Earth is in the middle scene of a three-act play. In Act I, a perfect world is created and then corrupted. In Act II, that corruption is played out while getting repaired. In Act III, the corruption is cleaned up and perfection restored. Judging the play by a brief glimpse of Act II is unreasonable. According to the Bible, which holds the script for the play, evil and suffering are only temporary. A day is coming when suffering will be wiped away, and evil will be no more. *"He has set a day for judging the world with justice..."*[14]

Why Let Suffering Continue?

Soon after the first Gulf War, a man named Richard came to my office. He said, "I want to know why God doesn't just wipe out Saddam Hussein and people like him in order to make the world a better place. People are dying. People are starving to death because of men like him. Why doesn't God just take those guys out?"

I knew some things about Richard. He had some struggles in his life, and he'd hurt some people along the way. He was concerned about the plight of the poor, but he had never done anything to personally help with it. I read him 2 Peter 3:9, *"The Lord is not slow in keeping his promise, as some understand slowness. He is patient with you, not wanting anyone to perish, but everyone to come to repentance."*

So I decided to give Richard a straight dose of truth. "Because of you," I said. "If God chose to intervene in history like that, you'd be 'taken out' too." He asked, "What do you mean?"

I replied, "Richard, God hasn't dealt with the evil in this world yet, because He wants to extend grace to you. God is delaying in His cleaning up of evil, in part, because He wants to give you a chance to have your sin forgiven rather than judged. He is far more troubled by the pain inflicted on people than you are. But He loves you so much, He's been holding off on bringing judgment. To be fair to all, on that day He'll have to judge you, and He'll have to judge me. And He doesn't want to judge you; He wants to give you grace instead." I then explained to Richard that grace was only a prayer away, that Christ paid for all the wrongs that he (Richard) and I had done

"He will wipe every tear from their eyes. There will be no more death or mourning or crying or pain, for the old order of things has passed away." Revelation 21:

to the world, and all we had to do was believe in Him and accept His payment and forgiveness.

The Full Story

The story of the world is the story of God and His perfect creation. He allowed for the possibility of evil and suffering by granting freedom of choice to His children. We chose to experience the evil and suffering (Act I). God then chose to make provision for our wrong choices by sending His Son to pay the penalty for them (Act II). This payment is available to all who will admit their need for it and trust Christ.

Because of the destructive power of evil, God will one day say, "Enough!" and judge the world, separating sin, evil and death from all that is good, and from those who have been forgiven of their evil by trusting in Christ (Act III). Paradise will then be fully restored in what the Bible calls *"the new heaven and the new earth,"* [15] in *"...a world where everyone is right with God."* [16]

The Best Part

The best part of the story is that all the pain and suffering of this world will seem insignificant compared to the pleasure we experience in heaven. Most of us have had our share of bumps and bruises in this life. Compare yours to those of the Apostle Paul:

> *I have worked harder, been put in jail more often, been whipped times without number, and faced death again and again. Five different times the Jews gave me thirty-nine lashes. Three times I was beaten with rods. Once I was stoned. Three times I was shipwrecked. Once I spent a whole night and a day adrift at sea. I have traveled many weary miles. I have faced danger from flooded rivers and*

from robbers. I have faced danger from my own people, the Jews, as well as from the Gentiles. I have faced dangers in cities, in the deserts, and on the stormy seas.... . I have lived with weariness and pain and sleepless nights. Often I have been hungry and thirsty and have gone without food. Often I have shivered with cold, without enough clothing to keep me warm.[17]

Yet, in the same letter, when Paul thinks about what he will experience in the life to come, he says, *"Our present troubles are quite small and won't last very long. Yet they produce for us an immeasurably great glory that will last forever!"*[18]

Suppose that on the first day of this year, you had a terrible day. You wake up with a migraine headache. At first, the pain is so bad that you're afraid you're going to die. Then it gets so bad, you *want* to die. On the way to the doctor's office, you are hit by an uninsured motorist, totaling your car. The car was a Christmas present, and it was the car you'd always dreamed of owning. Upon arriving at work, you find out that your company is downsizing, and your name is at the top of the list. The whole day goes like that — terrible.

Then the next day, you wake up to a phone call from a competitor offering you a better job with twice the pay. And suppose the entire rest of the year turns out like this. You inherit $1,000,000 from an unknown relative. You buy a lottery ticket with the first dollar, and you win another $10,000,000! Your children earn straight A's; they are so good, their teachers ask to take you to dinner because they want to meet the parent of such outstanding children. Your marriage is perfect. You get voted "Person of the Year" by the local newspaper. You play golf with Tiger Woods — and you win!

On December 31, someone asks you, "So, how was your year?" You answer, "It was unbelievable! Oh, yeah, that first day was a little rough, but everything else has gone so well, I had almost forgotten about it."

That's what it will be like in heaven.[19] That's Act III.

THINKING ABOUT IT

Something to Chew On:

The pain of this world holds no comparison to the pleasures of the one to come.

Verse to Remember:

"Now the dwelling place of God is with men, and he will live with them. They will be his people, and God himself will be with them and be their God. He will wipe every tear from their eyes. There will be no more death or mourning or crying or pain, for the old order of things has passed away." Revelation 21:4

Point to Ponder:

The conclusion of Act II will not only end pain and suffering, but it will also end my opportunity to respond to God's grace and to share it with others. How do I want to use the rest of the time I have in Act II, so I can maximize my experience in Act III?

My Thoughts on the Subject:

_____

_____

_____

_____

_____

_____

CAN A LOVING GOD REALLY SEND PEOPLE TO HELL?

"As the weeds are pulled up and burned in the fire, so it will be at the end of the age. The Son of Man will send out his angels, and they will weed out of his kingdom everything that causes sin and all who do evil."

Matthew 13:40

The Bible teaches that hell is a real place, and real people go there. It sounds almost savage, doesn't it? How could a loving God send anyone to hell? Could you imagine sentencing one of your children to eternal misery?

"Eternal misery," is a pretty good summary of hell. In the Bible, hell is called "an abyss," a place of darkness, condemnation, destruction, eternal fire, punishment, darkness, "weeping and gnashing of teeth." [20] It is truly a miserable place.

Why God Had to Create Hell

We live in a world of gradients. Some parts are good, and some are bad; others are in-between, but it's all relative. Now, imagine that all relativity is removed, so that things are only completely good or completely bad.

Completely good would be an apt description of heaven. It's the place where God dwells, so all is completely good, right, loving and beautiful, just like God Himself.

Now remove all the good. Imagine a place where there is only the *absence* of good. We have seen small examples of this in the ovens of Auschwitz and the killing fields of Cambodia. But even in those places, God was present, so a spark of good was resident there. Imagine no good and no God at all—that would be hell. Hell is the absence of God.

For Justice's Sake

God *had* to create hell, or He would not be just or loving. All groups and governments develop systems of justice, because human beings have an innate sense that evil cannot go unpunished. No one wants to live in a universe where the "Hitlers" get the same treatment as the "Mother Teresas." Evil must be paid for in order for there to be justice in the world. So God created hell, a place of eternal condemnation and destruction. It's the place where sin is paid for.

> *"The Lord is not slow in keeping his promise, as some understand slowness. He is patient with you, not wanting anyone to perish, but everyone to come to repentance."*
>
> 2 Peter 3:

I don't believe that God *wanted* to create hell. His justice demanded it. He could not remain who He was—a just, moral being—without making provision for the payment of sin. So having created hell, God did everything He could to prevent any of His children from going there. He spared no expense, giving the life of His innocent Son to pay for the sins of the world. And He invites everyone to have their sins paid for by Christ's death.

But if God is going to allow each of His children to have true free will, He cannot force His forgiveness on any of us. Once again, He must allow us to choose for ourselves. So God says, "Choose. Sin must be paid for in order for there to be justice. You can pay it yourself, or I will pay it for you." Without hell, humans would have no true choice, because there would be no real and final consequences for our actions. When a mother says to her son, "If you touch one more cookie before you finish your dinner, I'll have to send you to your room," and the boy stuffs another cookie in his mouth, what's the one thing Mom must do? Send him to his room. Otherwise she loses her trustworthiness, respectability and authority. The same is true with God; He must enforce the moral rules of the universe, or He Himself would be immoral.

Because of Love

Imagine living in a world where fire is supposed to burn us, but it never does. Every time we reach our hand toward a flame, the flame goes out. Imagine living in a world where you couldn't experience any thrills, because every time you strapped on a set of skis or paddled out to a giant wave or jumped out of an airplane, the laws of Nature were suspended. Imagine living in a world where every time you got mad at someone, it became physically impossible to express your anger. Psychologists have designed such a place; it's called a "padded cell."

God knew we couldn't be truly free if He created only a padded-cell world. So He created a world in which His children could explore, experience, make choices and have their actions count. God loved His children so much that He wanted them to be able to choose to love Him or not. So when the first humans sinned, God made provision for justice by the sacrifice of His Son. He said,

"Come to me." Though the gap between us and God was huge, God bridged it. He came all the way to our planet and then into our hearts, whispering, "I love you, child. Come to Me."

Suppose some of His children refuse His invitation? Suppose they shake their bony fists at God and say, "I don't want to be forgiven! I don't want to have a relationship with You! I want nothing to do with You!" For God to continue to love, He must give these children the consequences of their choice. He must give them a place that is absent from His presence.

What would a place that had no trace of God in it be like? Think of all the things that God is: loving, just, hope-filled, beautiful, in-community,[21] significant, purposeful, etc. Now imagine a place where all of those qualities are absent: no love, no justice, no hope, no beauty, no community, no significance and no purpose. When you remove all of God from a place, it becomes a place of torment and anguish. There is "weeping and gnashing of teeth" because it's a place of regret. That's hell.

Summary

For God to truly love His children, He had to make provision for them to choose to live without Him for eternity. In effect, God is saying, "I did not create evil, but I allowed for it so that you could have the freedom to choose between right and wrong, and the freedom to love Me. I don't like suffering, but I can make good come from it. Suffering won't always be part of the world. But for now, when you are in pain, know that I will be with you. I will hold your hand. I will walk with you in sorrow, if you will let Me. Someday I will wipe it away once and for all. Someday your bliss will be so strong that your present suffering won't be worth comparing to it."

THINKING ABOUT IT

Something to Chew On:

Hell is a real place, and it's the last place God wants His children to go.

Verse to Remember:

"Enter through the narrow gate. For wide is the gate and broad is the road that leads to destruction, and many enter through it." Matthew 7:13

Point to Ponder:

Have I chosen to ask Christ to forgive my sin, or am I planning to pay for it myself?

My Thoughts on the Subject:

Sabbath

A Day of Rest

Jesus' invitation, *"Come to me, all you who are weary and burdened, and I will give you rest."* (Luke 11:28) is an invitation not only to rest on the Sabbath, but to find your rest in Him. Attend church today and let the people, songs, sermon and change of pace rejuvenate your soul.

END NOTES

WHAT ARE THE POSSIBILITIES?
1. Job 4:7.
2. Job 15:20.
3. Job 20:5.
4. Job 42:3, 6.

DID GOD CREATE EVIL?
5. Genesis 2:16-17.
6. Genesis 1:31.
7. Romans 5:12, NLT.
8. Romans 8:22, NLT.

WHAT'S THE POINT OF PROBLEMS?
9. Proverbs 20:30, TEV.
10. James 1:2-3, NCV.
11. Psalm 119:71, LB.
12. Romans 5:3-4, LB.

WHAT KIND OF ANSWER DO YOU NEED?
13. 1 Corinthians 2:9.

WHICH ACT ARE WE LIVING IN?
14. Acts 17:31, NLT.
15. Revelation 21:1.
16. 2 Peter 3:13.
17. 2 Corinthians 11:23-27, NLT.
18. 2 Corinthians 4:17, NLT.
19. We are indebted to a sermon by Lee Strobel for this concept.

CAN A LOVING GOD REALLY SEND PEOPLE TO HELL?
20. See Revelation 1:9; Matthew 8:10; Matthew 23:23; John 3:18; Romans 9:22; Matthew 25:41; Matthew 25:46; Jude 13.
21. God is an eternal community of Three: Father, Son and Holy Spirit.

Other Great Questions

Almost all of the questions people have ever asked about God and Christianity can be summarized in eight categories: four major and four minor.

THE MAJOR GOD QUESTIONS:

- How can I know if God is real?
- How can I know if the Bible is true?
- Aren't all religions basically the same?
- If God is so good and so great, why does He allow suffering in the world?

Now that we've spent several days exploring the major questions, let's spend the remainder of this study examining the minor questions.

THE MINOR GOD QUESTIONS:

- Isn't Christianity a crutch for weak people?
- Will God send to hell those who have never heard of Jesus?
- If the church is so great, why is it full of hypocrites?
- What happens to me when I die?

ISN'T CHRISTIANITY
A CRUTCH
FOR WEAK PEOPLE?

"He never left himself without a witness. There were always his reminders, such as sending you rain and good crops and giving you food and joyful hearts."

Acts 14:17, NLT

One summer during college, I traveled in Europe with a few friends. While walking uphill to the fortress in Salzburg, Austria, I struck up a conversation with two of my fellow travelers: John from Wisconsin, and Francois from Quebec. John was a sincere spiritual seeker, and our conversation quickly turned to Christ and Christianity. Before it went far, though, Francois couldn't contain himself. "What are you talking about?" he blurted out. "Don't you know that religion is just a crutch for people who can't handle the truth?" "What do you mean?" John asked.

Francois answered, "I mean, there is no God, there is no spiritual world. They're just inventions of tiny people who couldn't stand the thought that they might be all alone in the universe and that their lives might end at the grave. Christianity and other religious constructs are just fairy tales people made up around campfires to help them sleep at night."

Francois isn't the first person to hold this belief. Karl Marx believed that religion was an attractive escape-mechanism for the downtrodden and depressed. Sigmund Freud believed that humans in the past dealt with the threat of the forces of Nature by personal-

"Religion is the opiate of the people." Karl Marx

izing them: If we can make the wind or rain or volcanoes into a god, we can reason with them. And if we can reason with them, maybe we can persuade them to show mercy.

The Apostle Paul observed that many people find reasons not to believe in God. He said, *"... the truth about God is known to them instinctively. God has put this knowledge in their hearts. From the time the world was created, people have seen the earth and sky and all that God made. They can clearly see his invisible quali-ties—his eternal power and divine nature. So they have no excuse whatsoever for not knowing God."* [1]

Two Problems

As we have seen over the last several weeks, Christianity has many objective, tangible proofs about such things as the existence of God, the reality of the incarnation, the resurrection of Christ and the historical evidence of the Bible. It's not a made-up system of psychological smoke-and-mirrors; it's a truth system based on fact, logic and experience. If an argument can be made that people *in-vented* the idea of God for fear that there might be *nothing out there*, a stronger argument can be made that people have tried to *un-invent* the idea of God for fear that there might be *SOMETHING* out there.

For many people, the idea that there *is a* God can present a bigger threat than the idea that there *is no* God. Most of us spend a fair amount of time trying to hide certain things about ourselves so that others will think well of us. If there is a God, and He is all-knowing, then there is no hiding. He knows everything about us. Most of us also want to have control of our lives, but if there is a God who governs the universe, then there goes our control, including the control of our eternal destiny. Statistically, driving is more dangerous than flying, yet people fear flying. Why? Because we don't get to control the airplane.

Perhaps the biggest threat that God presents is the threat to our pride. We don't like the thought that someone might have "power over us." If God is real, He not only has power over us, He has *absolute* power over us. In the Old Testament, a young man named Isaiah saw a vision of God.[2] The reality of God was so powerful that Isaiah said, *"Woe is me! I am ruined!"*[3] When Isaiah saw himself in comparison to God, it made him realize things about himself that were hard to face.

Is Christianity a crutch for people who can't handle the idea that there might be no power in the universe that can help us? Or is atheism a crutch for people who can't handle the idea that there might be a Divine Power in the universe that can judge us?

THINKING ABOUT IT

Something to Chew On:

For some people, believing there is a God can be more of a threat than believing there is no God.

Verse to Remember:

"...he never left himself without a witness. There were always his reminders, such as sending you rain and good crops and giving you food and joyful hearts." Acts 14:17, NLT

Point to Ponder:

Which is easier: believing there is a God I will have to answer to one day, or believing I am accountable to no one?

My Thoughts on the Subject:

WHAT ABOUT THOSE WHO'VE NEVER HEARD ABOUT JESUS?

"The Lord...is patient with you, not wanting anyone to perish, but everyone to come to repentance."

2 Peter 3:9

As a freshman in college, my dormitory floor was mostly populated by young men from Iran. Before that year, I had never met anyone of Persian descent, nor had I the opportunity to cultivate friendships with individuals whose faith tradition differed from my own. As I began to form relationships with these students, I would ask if they had ever been exposed to the message of Christ. Many admitted that they'd had very little exposure to the Christian faith; often they had come to the United States in search of a quality education and planned to return to Iran after graduation. I liked these guys and enjoyed their company, but I didn't know how to reconcile my Christian faith with their Islamic faith.

Moreover, I was bothered by the position that Jesus took in the New Testament book of John. In verse 14:6, Jesus said, *"I am the way, the truth and the life. No one can come to the Father except through me."* I realized that this verse seemed to exclude my new friends from eternal life. It's one thing to consider this verse in theory, but quite another to process it in light of real people who I had grown to know and love. But what bothered me the most was that these young men had not been given the same opportunity that I had to hear or understand the Gospel of Jesus, so how could they be held accountable for it?

In an effort to resolve this conflict, I decided to take a comparative religion class at the university I was attending. I hoped to find answers, but the class only caused me more confusion. Ironically, the crux of the dilemma came from the very words of Jesus Himself. He had made such a strong statement about salvation that it seemed there was no room for those who had never heard about him.

"As humans we long to create a belief system where all roads lead heaven, because we long for that t be true; the truth remains that noth ing in the created order works that way. All roads don't lead to Miami. In fact, only a very few roads will actually take you to Miami. Most roads lead elsewhere." Dan Grider

Making Himself Known

One day as I was reading Scripture, I discovered a passage in Romans that helped me find peace with my dilemma. Paul explains that each person has the ability to respond to God. In verse 1:19, Paul addresses the issue of people who have never heard the message of Christ. He says, *"What may be known about God is plain to them, because God has made it plain to them. For since the creation of the world God's invisible qualities, his eternal power and divine nature have been clearly seen, being understood from what has been made, so that people are without excuse."*[4]

It appears that God holds all of us accountable to respond to Him in a way that is aligned with our level of understanding of who God is. It says that all people are without excuse. Each of us must seek a relationship with God. The Bible indicates that God is most interested in our willingness to obey Him. For example, in 1 Samuel 15:22, Samuel says obedience is better than sacrifice. God is looking for people who will respond via relational obedience rather than in an impersonal, ritualistic way.

The passage from Romans is prefaced with this: *"The wrath of God is being revealed from heaven against all the godlessness and wickedness of men who suppress the truth by their wickedness."*[5] Paul is warning us against blindly following a religion that suppresses the truth about the life-giving message of Christ. To do so would in fact be a rejection of all that Jesus did on our behalf. Here our problem is not one of lacking information; rather, it is one of willing rebellion—a lack of willingness to obey God's commands. Paul continues, saying,

> *"...they exchanged the truth of God for a lie, and worshiped and served created things rather than the Creator"...*[6] We are reminded that, *"since the creation of the world God's invisible qualities—his eternal power and divine nature—have been clearly seen, being understood from what has been made, so that men are without excuse. For although they knew God, they neither glorified him as God nor gave thanks to him, but their thinking became futile and their foolish hearts were darkened. Although they claimed to be wise, they became fools."*[7]

God calls every one of us, regardless of culture or religion, to respond to Him. The Bible says that we are responsible to respond to God at the level of our revelation, and all of us are without excuse. Obviously, a person who has received the full knowledge of Christ has become responsible to respond to the message of Jesus as the Bible reveals. However, a person who does not have an understanding of the message of Christ is only responsible to respond at the level of the revelation received, even if it is limited.

For instance, anyone who has lived in a remote area of the jungle, having never experienced anything beyond ancestor worship or superstitious responses, is still responsible in their heart to respond to God as He has revealed Himself in the created order. This allows them to still come to Christ, even though they've never heard of Christ. They must respond to God as dictated by their own revelation of the Almighty.

It appears then that God has not left Himself without a witness, for the book of Romans says that even the created order is the witness of Christ. When people know of Christ, and yet reject Him or the knowledge of Him, they have in effect rejected God's provision for them.

It is not wise to have the knowledge of Jesus Christ and His saving message and still adhere to the belief that all roads lead to heaven. Jesus never taught that this was a possibility. The Scripture says no one comes to the Father but by Him.

Imagine you took a trip to a national park with a group of friends. You began the day with great expectations and with the joy of seeing the beauty of the natural surroundings. But as the day continued, you became increasingly aware that you had lost your orientation. The group's joy came to a halt when everyone began to discuss the correct way back to the car. Everyone agreed the car was north, but each of you disagreed about which way was north.

Now let's say you had a compass with you. Even though everyone was adamantly declaring their particular direction as correct, you would not be considered hateful or intolerant if you shared with them your knowledge. The car is only in one location; the car cannot be in six locations. You possess a compass, which can direct you back in accuracy to true north, to exactly the place where the car is located.

Likewise, the truth of the message of Christ is uniquely different from the message of all other world religions. Even Jesus in His time was said to be One who was able to speak with authority, not like the religious teachers of the period. And so, just as knowing the true direction with the aid of a compass is not a bad or hateful thing, knowing the direction that God has given us is a beautiful revelation from God Himself.

Jesus clearly said that all roads do not lead to heaven. He said, *"Enter through the narrow gate. For wide is the gate and broad is the road that leads to destruction, and many enter through it. But small is the gate and narrow the road that leads to life, and only a few find it."*

Every person who has wrestled with the question of the fate of non-believers does so because they need to believe that God plays fair. But the Bible is clear that we each have God's fingerprint placed on our hearts, and we have an inherent moral obligation to respond to Him.

THINKING ABOUT IT

Something to Chew On:

The concern is not "What about those who have never heard?" but rather, "What am I going to do now that I have heard?"

Verse to Remember:

"The Lord is not slow in keeping his promise, as some understand slowness. He is patient with you, not wanting anyone to perish, but everyone to come to repentance." 2 Peter 3:9

Point to Ponder:

Do I believe that God has revealed Himself to everyone on earth in a way to which every person can respond?

My Thoughts on the Subject:

IF CHRISTIANITY IS TRUE, WHY IS THE CHURCH FULL OF HYPOCRITES?

"How can you think of saying, 'Friend, let me help you get rid of that speck in your eye,' when you can't see past the log in your own eye? Hypocrite! First get rid of the log from your own eye; then perhaps you will see well enough to deal with the speck in your friend's eye."

Luke 6:42, NLT

Most people can't stand hypocrisy. Our stomachs roil when we see a leader stand up and say one thing and then do another. The stench of hypocrisy not only sours us to people, but to their position as well.

Karl Marx was born into a long line of devout Jews. His father, Heinrich, was a well-respected Jewish lawyer in the Prussian city of Trier. Heinrich's father and grandfather were both rabbis. As Trier's economic climate changed, Heinrich's clients exited the city for employment elsewhere. In order to preserve his business, Heinrich abandoned the Jewish faith and joined the Lutheran church.

Karl believed that his father was a hypocrite, leaving one faith system for another not out of conviction but for expediency. For the rest of Marx's life, this feeling that his father had acted hypocritically left him with a negative impression of both his father and his father's new religion.[8]

We all know someone who attends church on Sundays and "lives like hell" the rest of the week. How can this be? If Christianity is true, how can people who claim to be Christians lie to their friends, cheat in their businesses, treat others harshly and generally do things that are mean and nasty?

Three Responses

The Church *Should Be* Full of Hypocrites

Jesus founded His church to bring people into relationship with God and to help them become more like God. The one trait common to all Christians is their admission that they need God's help with their lives. So if a church is doing what God wants, it will be attracting people who look and act like they need a Savior.

Does this excuse arrogant, immature or hypocritical behavior by church members? By no means! But maybe it does explain it. If a church is doing its job right, people with problems will feel free to enter into the life of that church and bring all their baggage with them. Hopefully, over time, as God

"Hyp-o-crite (hyp'e krit) n. an actor; person who pretends to be what he not; one who pretends to be better he really is, or to be pious, virtuous etc., without really being so."

Webster's New World Dict

heals their wounds, their baggage will shrink. This has certainly been the case in our church. One of my greatest joys is watching new believers making progress in their faith. Often, as growing believers realize God's love for them, they will turn around and love others more authentically. Almost always, people who get forgiven ask forgiveness and admit their shortcomings to those they've wounded.

Not All Christians are Hypocrites

Many of the Christians I know are the most authentic people I know. For instance, I ate lunch recently with a young lady named Julie. Julie is a single mother raising four children by herself. Her past includes some very harsh treatment by her father, and some equally harsh treatment by her former husband. Whether because of these relationships or simple heredity, Julie suffers from depression.

In the past, Julie attempted to escape her pain by drinking. A few years ago, she gave her life to Christ. Since that day, Julie has become a model of authenticity. Because she knows that she's been forgiven, she doesn't feel the need to pretend about her past or even about her struggles with depression. Since she met Christ, she has become as honest as any person I know. Even in the midst of her own struggles, Julie has "adopted" an elderly couple that lives across the street from our church. Besides caring for her four children, she cares for this family as well. Julie is the first to admit she's not perfect, but she is a perfect example of the love of Christ transforming someone.

Jesus Was Not a Hypocrite

The ultimate issue about Christianity is the person of Jesus. If Jesus was a hypocrite, then following Him makes no sense at all. But throughout the New Testament, Jesus' detractors admitted that they could find no hypocrisy in Jesus. At His trial, the Bible says, "The chief priests and the whole Sanhedrin were looking for false evidence against Jesus so that they could put him to death. But they did not find any, though many false witnesses came forward." (Matthew 26:59-60) The Roman governor who presided at His trial said, "I find no basis for a charge against him." (John 18:38) Jesus' words and actions matched perfectly. It is because of His absolute lack of hypocrisy that the Church exists and is worth joining.

Jesus often warned the disciples against judging others before reflecting on their own capacity to sin. Luke 6:42 cautions us against making broad statements about groups of people based on one or a few examples. If someone was to judge the human race by your daily behavior alone, would it reflect humanity well? Or even accurately? Before deciding that "all Christians are..." or "the church is full of...", consider how often you fall short or poorly represent your personal values. And once you do, celebrate, because Christ welcomes you anyway—shortcomings and all—and so should His church.

THINKING ABOUT IT

Something to Chew On:

While most people detest hypocrisy, none of us would be eligible to join any organization that keeps hypocrites out.

Verse to Remember:

"Above all, my brothers, do not swear—not by heaven or by earth or by anything else. Let your 'Yes' be yes, and your 'No,' no, or you will be condemned." James 5:12

Point to Ponder:

How well do my words match my deeds? On a scale of 1 to 10, what's my own hypocrisy quotient?

My Thoughts on the Subject:

WHAT HAPPENS TO ME WHEN I DIE?

"...and the dust returns to the ground it came from, and the spirit returns to God who gave it."

Ecclesiastes 12:7

There comes a point in each person's life when we ask on some dark night, "Is this life all there is?" It's a valid and profound question, and one we don't often share. Instead, we ponder it privately in our hearts.

With the rise of spirituality in the late 1990s and early 2000s, interest in life after death is at an all-time high. Bookstores offer dozens of titles that describe afterlife scenarios. Anecdotes recounting mysterious out-of-body experiences have become commonplace. Interestingly, most of the stories we hear have happy endings. But some near-death stories describe a much darker encounter.

In his research on near-death encounters, Dr. Maurice Rawlings found that just about half of the people who experience out-of-body encounters have a vision of hell instead of a vision of heaven. These darker stories don't usually make the press, but they are equally significant. Rawlings found that many people were so unsettled by their near-death encounter that they did not want to talk about it. In fact, they struggled to deal with the experience at all.

Our interest in the afterlife says some positive things about our culture. First, it says we're thinking about what comes next. Thinking precedes preparation; that's a good thing. Second, if these documented experiences are true, it indicates that there *is* life after death. This is good news, but it leads to something that worries me. People I know and love plan to spend eternity in heaven, but they are not necessarily consulting with *God* about those plans. In fact, some are leaving "the God of heaven" out of their lives altogether.

> *"We don't see things as they are, we see them as we are."*
>
> Anais Nin

In the 1970s and 80s, many baby-boomers acted as if, by ignoring aging, they could perhaps also ignore their mortality. But in the end, Mark Twain had it right: There are only two things we can be sure of in this life, *death and taxes*. Death is no respecter of persons, regardless of how wealthy, old, beautiful or powerful we are. None of us can avoid it.

According to the Bible, death is the dividing line between this life and "eternity." Compared to eternity, this life is like a fading flower or withering grass. [9] Smart investors put their assets into the thing that will last.

Jesus: The Eternal Expert

Jesus spoke more about eternity than did all of the other Biblical writers combined. He is, after all, the only One able to speak about eternity from personal experience. He also personally knows the joy of being with the Father in a complete relationship in the eternal realms even before the beginning of time. The Bible says that after his crucifixion, Jesus *"...descended to the lower, earthly regions."* [10] Jesus experienced the devastating loneliness and isolation of being separated from the Father during and just after his death on the cross. Jesus is the *only* expert on the subject of eternity. Jesus spoke warnings about living well, so that we would be prepared for eternity. He taught about this topic from a position of love. Jesus taught that we have a loving Father who desires an eternal relationship with us and a fulfillment of the purpose to which we have been called—to glorify Him. Jesus said, *"I desire that they ... may be with me ... and that they may behold my glory."* [11]

Jesus often taught about heaven and hell. His references to heaven were not so much about palatial cities of grandeur and beauty, but as a place of being in relationship with Him and His Father.

Two Kinds of Death

The Bible teaches that there are two kinds of death: The first is a physical death; the second death is an eternal, spiritual death. Jesus cautioned us to be more concerned about the second death than the first. He warns, *"Do not be afraid of those who kill the body but cannot kill the soul. Rather, be afraid of the one who can destroy both soul and body in hell."* [12]

Jesus' teachings on the subject of hell were graphic and visual. He made reference to a place near the ancient city of Jerusalem known as Gehenna. It was located outside the city wall and was the place where the city's trash would burn and smolder without ever being extinguished. From the vantage point of Gehenna, you would probably be able to look up and see the activities of life in the city. However, since no one could scale the slippery, spring-fed, mossy rock walls around the city, this point of view would most likely make you feel trapped and lonely. So from the perspective of Gehenna, one would require no further explanation of how unpleasant and isolated hell will be. By the reference, Jesus was indicating that those who choose to live separately from God in the physical life will remain lonely and separated from Him in the afterlife.

Jesus further illustrates the nature of eternity in a story of two very different men. The first owned much, and the second owned little. The wealthy man was possessed by his possessions and was concerned about finding pleasure in life. The poor man ate the breadcrumbs from the rich man's table. At the time, it was customary for wealthy people to wipe their hands on bread like napkins and then dispose of the bread by tossing it from the table. The poor would come after the meal and eat the bread that the wealthy had tossed away.

Eventually, both rich and poor men die and are faced with two very different eternities. The poor man, because of his priorities, had inherited God's eternity. By no means does this story imply that Jesus condemns riches; however, he does caution us not to become so busy accumulating things that we have no time for God. Jesus also distinguishes between the place of eternal comfort and the place of eternal torment and separation, and He clearly reminds us that after we die, there are only two alternatives.

In our popular culture where everything is relative, many people do not accept this teaching of Jesus. People prefer to believe that heaven exists, but they deny the existence of hell, or they assume it is simply a temporary place of penance. Many who believe in heaven cut-and-paste it together with mythological icons such as clouds, angel wings and harps.

The Choice is Yours

Jesus' teaching about the nature of heaven and hell was not intended to scare us; it was meant to teach us how to live. Imagine you and I were driving and saw a sign warning that a bridge ahead was unsafe. Would we speed up, ignoring the people and signs trying to stop us from driving across the bridge? If we refused to stop despite the advice, we would be responsible for our own deaths. God has warned us that this life and the decisions we make in this life are serious matters. We will go to one of two destinies in eternity, and we are each fully responsible for our eternal destination. Author C.S. Lewis said, "Hell is locked from the inside. The residents of hell have chosen the outcome of hell with intention and clarity." [13]

The benefit of accepting Christ as our Savior is that we can live without fear. Jesus told us that we do not know the time of His return, so we should live our lives prepared for it. He said, *"No one knows about that day or hour, not even the angels in heaven, nor the Son, but only the Father."* (Matthew 24:36)

Because we do not know when that day will come, we certainly do not know if we can afford to wait to make a decision to follow Christ. None of us can be certain when the end of our life will be. Jesus tells us to prepare now.

God has taken considerable steps to ensure that we have an eternal choice. Jesus came to offer us the gift of eternal life in heaven. We must turn from our ways and yield to Him to redeem the offer. I invite you to take this all-important step now. Simply ask God to come into your life through the presence of the Holy Spirit. It is as simple as pausing now, bowing your head and whispering the prayer that can change your eternity:

> *Jesus, I know that You are the answer I've been looking for. I will follow You, and I receive You as my life director. Thank You for saving me and making me perfect. Thank you for preparing a place for me to be with You in heaven. In Your name, I pray. Amen.*

If you have taken this all-important step, I want to rejoice with you and welcome you to the family of God and to your eternal destiny! The next step is to tell someone about your decision. This is the beginning of a life with God and His family.

THINKING ABOUT IT

Something to Chew On:

Think about your concept of eternal life. Begin to sort through the ideas that are not Biblical. Try to lay emotion aside and replace them with the truth of Scripture.

Verse to Remember:

"Why, you do not even know what will happen tomorrow. What is your life? You are a mist that appears for a little while and then vanishes. Instead, you ought to say, 'If it is the Lord's will, we will live and do this or that.'" James 4:14-15

Point to Ponder:

Are you certain about your eternal destiny? If not, what will you do about it?

My Thoughts on the Subject:

DOES GOD CHANGE?

*"All men are like grass, and all their glory
is like the flowers of the field. The grass withers
and the flowers fall... but the word
of our God stands forever."*

Isaiah 40:6-8

I had a thought one day: What if we woke up and the world was completely different? What if suddenly the things we knew about the universe weren't true anymore? What if gravity wasn't in force? Or, if the things we are used to eating were now poisonous, and the things that were poisonous were edible? What if the world were completely unpredictable? This led to a deeper question: what if *God* were unpredictable? What kind of world would it be if there was literally NOTHING we could count on? Sounds a bit like hell, doesn't it? In fact, if hell is the absence of God, maybe that's partially what it will be like.

This begs another question: What if God were *deliberately unpredictable*? What if He were secretly manipulative, holding us inside a warped fantasy, and one day He'll turn on all of us? The world would be a cosmic nightmare. We would all walk around completely paranoid. If God can't be trusted or if God can change, then there is no anchor to the universe, nothing to which we can trust or hold.

Thankfully, God is nothing like that. He is completely trustworthy, and He always will be, because He never changes. The Bible says, *"Jesus Christ is the same yes-terday and today and forever."* [14] Scholars have a word for this charac-teristic; it's called His *"immutability."* (In nickel-sized words, it means "not-able-to-mutate.") We don't think about it much, but this characteristic of immutability means that, once we've figured out the big questions in life (who God is, what our purpose

> *"Men sometimes say things they do not really mean, simply because they do not know their own mind; also, because their views change, they frequently find that they can no longer stand to things that they said in the past... But not so with the words of God. They stand forever..."*
>
> J.I. Packer, Knowing God

is while on earth, etc.), those things will never change, because God will never change. In other words, what you now know as *true truth about truth* will never change. Now that you know what God is like, you can count on Him to ALWAYS be like that. As many people have found, and as we will read in the next chapter, our purpose here on earth involves worship, fellowship, dis-cipleship, service and evangelism. When you discover these things, you can build your life with confidence around them because they are true and truth, like God.

Here's another 50-cent word: *"aseity."* You won't find it in your standard dictionary, and if you type it on your computer, your spell-checker will reject it (which makes it a really cool word, because you can use it to im-press your friends). *Aseity* means "self-existent." Part of why God never changes is because He is completely self-existent. He doesn't age; He doesn't experience entropy.

Basically, God has no needs, which is exceptionally wonderful! What if God had needs? What if God needed something from *you*? If He did, it would be difficult to trust Him; if He didn't get what He needed from you, He could overwhelm you and take it by force. There would be nothing to restrain Him from doing so.

Fortunately, God needs nothing from you. He *wants* your love, loyalty and service. He *wants* your friendship. He *wants* to give you all sorts of wonderful things, like purpose and fulfillment and hope. But He "needs" nothing. He is absolutely trustworthy because of His self-sufficiency.

Not many people ask the question, "Does God change?" because we intuitively know that if He did, this world would look far different (far darker) than it is. *Immutability* and *aseity* are two very big words, and very big qualities of God, for which we can be very grateful.

THINKING ABOUT IT

Something to Chew On:

God never changes; therefore, the world is predictable, and He is trustworthy.

Verse to Remember:

"All that I know now is partial and incomplete, but then I will know everything completely, just as God knows me now." 1 Corinthians 13:12, NLT

Point to Ponder:

If God answered every question I have, would that be a good thing? Or, for now, are there some things better left unknown?

My Thoughts on the Subject:

WHAT'S THE PURPOSE OF THE CHURCH?

"I will build my church, and the gates of Hades shall not overcome it."

Matthew 16:18

The most important question of our lives is "Why am I here?" or "What's my purpose?" You and I cannot understand the answer to these questions unless we understand the church.

In my humble opinion, the church is the most misunderstood institution in the world. Ask your typical person on the street, "What's a church?" and you'll likely hear a description of a building somewhere that holds religious services. Ask another person on the street, "What is the purpose of the church?" and you'll likely hear one of the following: "To worship God." "To help people." "To help the needy." All of those are good answers; they're just not full answers.

Ask a typical member of a church, "Why does your church exist?" and you'll likely hear, "To help me grow spiritually." "To meet my needs." "To help me spiritually educate my children." Ask God that same question, and you'll get a very different answer.

The Bible describes the church as Christ's bride.[15] It tells us that right now, in heaven, Jesus is praying for

His church.[16] To God, the church is the most important institution in the world. All of His plans are about its success. All of His hopes for eternity are wrapped up in it. All of His efforts since the Fall in Genesis 3 are about building His eternal family, which Jesus named "The church." [17]

Throughout the New Testament there are six snapshots of what the church is. God calls it:

- A building [18]
- A body [19]
- A family [20]
- An army [21]
- A flock [22]
- A bride [23]

A building is solid and useful. A body is fluid and living. A family is organic and relational (and sometimes quirky). An army has a mission and is strategic. A flock is dependent. A bride prepares and can't wait to celebrate. Separately, none of these images is an adequate description of what God had in mind when He created the church.

"The local church is the hope of the world."
Bill Hybels

In God's mind, the church is a complex wonder; He can't describe it in just one or two words or images. But if you put all six of these images together, you begin to get the full picture of what the church is all about. The New Testament book of Acts describes the very first church. It describes it not by what it was, but rather by what it *did*.

They devoted themselves to the apostles' teaching and to the fellowship, to the breaking of bread and to prayer. Everyone was filled with awe, and many wonders and miraculous signs were done by the apostles. All the believers were together and had everything in common. Selling their possessions and goods, they gave to anyone as he had need. Every day they continued to meet together in the temple courts. They broke bread in their homes and ate together with glad and sincere hearts, praising God and enjoying the favor of all the people. And the Lord added to their number daily those who were being saved. [24]

Best-selling author and pastor Rick Warren has helped us see that the church has five purposes:

- Worship ("They devoted themselves to...the breaking of bread and to prayer.")

- Fellowship ("They devoted themselves to...the fellowship.")

- Discipleship ("They devoted themselves to the apostles' teaching...")

- Service ("They gave to anyone as he had need...")

- Evangelism ("The Lord added to their number daily those who were being saved.")

These five purposes just happen to be the very five purposes for which God put people here on earth. We are to worship Him, get to know and grow with the church, serve in the church and share the Good News of Christ with the world.

Is it a coincidence that the people's purpose and the church's purpose are one and the same? Everything you've learned in this study was designed for you to put to use in your life, in the building of Christ's church, in one or more of these five ways. What does that look like for you today? How are you worshiping? And how well are you doing it? With whom are you fellowshipping, and how are they benefiting from what you're putting into their life?

Hopefully the answers you've received during this study have helped you grow. What will you do with what you now know in order to build Christ's church? In what ways are you serving the church? With whom are you sharing the Good News, or are you praying for a chance to share it? 1 Corinthians 8:1 says, *"Knowledge puffs up, but love builds up."* What will you do with the knowledge you've gained so that it doesn't just swell your head?

THINKING ABOUT IT

Something to Chew On:

Every one of God's purposes for you is related to the building up of His church.

Verse to Remember:

"I will build my church, and the gates of Hades will not overcome it." Matthew 16:18

Point to Ponder:

What's your purpose in the church?

My Thoughts on the Subject:

_____

_____

_____

_____

_____

_____

Sabbath

A Day of Rest

Yesterday you read about the six images of the church in the New Testament. Attend church today as a restful change of pace, and while you're there, see which image or images you experience:

- The church as a building.
- The church as a body.
- The church as a family.
- The church as an army.
- The church as a flock.
- The church as a bride.

See you tomorrow!

END NOTES

ISN'T CHRISTIANITY A CRUTCH FOR WEAK PEOPLE?
1. Romans 1:19-20, NLT.
2. Isaiah 6:1-10.
3. Isaiah 6:5.

WHAT ABOUT THOSE WHO'VE NEVER HEARD ABOUT JESUS?
4. Romans 1:19-20.
5. Romans 1:18.
6. Romans 1:25.
7. Romans 1:20-22.

IF CHRISTIANITY IS TRUE, WHY IS THE CHURCH FULL OF HYPOCRITES?
8. As told in Sproul, *Reason to Believe*, p. 84.

WHAT HAPPENS TO ME WHEN I DIE?
9. Psalm 103:15.
10. Ephesians 4:8-9.
11. John 17:24.
12. Matthew 10:28.
13. Boa and Moody, *I'm Glad You Asked*, p. 145.

DOES GOD CHANGE?
14. Hebrews 13:8.

WHAT'S THE PURPOSE OF THE CHURCH?
15. Revelation 19:7.
16. Romans 8:34.
17. Matthew 16:18.
18. Ephesians 2:20.
19. Ephesians 4:15-16.
20. Ephesians 2:19.
21. Ephesians 6:12.
22. 1 Peter 5:2.
23. Revelation 19:7.
24. Acts 2:42-47.

Closing Questions

WHAT'S THE PURPOSE
OF MY LIFE?

*"The Lord has made everything
for His own purposes."*

Proverbs 16:4 NLT

Several years ago, I was working as an announcer at a secular radio station in the Midwest. We were in a rather large city with a diverse population. I was live on the air, and one caller phoned in with a most unusual comment. He said that the only way to have purpose in life was through Jesus, and until the listeners took that step they would always be frustrated and living below their potential. He concluded by saying that the only way to understand our life purpose is to consult the One who created us. We were discussing a totally separate topic; however, I loved his boldness and perspective, and I wholeheartedly agreed with him.

I was flooded with different thoughts of how I should respond. I wanted to shift the entire program to the topic. I felt a sense of camaraderie with the caller who wanted my listeners to know God's purpose for their lives. I chose to affirm him and continue the show. But the caller hit a nerve with my listeners. I didn't have to shift the focus of the program; my listeners did it for me. It was amazing how many people wanted to know more about how to find their God-given purpose and direction for their life.

I suggested that if you were confused about the operation or purpose of a device, the best approach would be
to consult the owner's manual. I added that the reason
God gave us the Bible was to
teach us what our life purpose
is. I also advised, "If you want to
know why a device was made,
you should consult the Creator
of the device." As an example,

*"Surely God would not have
created such a being as man*
exist for a day! No, no, man w
made for immortality."

Abraham Lir

I said that I'd recently gone to an estate auction. While
there, I stumbled across some strange-looking gadgets
and gizmos. "Those gadgets looked strange to me, but the
owner knew exactly what they were for," I said.

God has also fashioned you for a distinct purpose.
He carefully crafted you to fulfill a part of His plan for all
of creation. He planned who you would become and how
long you would live. He designed your inquisitive mind.
Even the way that you have wrestled with your own set
of "God Questions" is a part of how God made you. No
part of who you are is a mistake. The Bible reminds me
that God "knew me before I was born and scheduled each
day of my life before I began to breathe. Every day was
recorded in His book!"[1] This is the amazing truth that
comes from our owner's manual (the Bible).

God's plan also takes into consideration our unique
talents and gifts. The Bible tells us *"that we are God's
workmanship created in Christ Jesus to do good works,
which God prepared in advance that we should do."*[2]
God does not simply leave His plan as a casual take-it-
or-leave-it affair. He expects us to fully embrace it. He
means business.

The apostle Paul said it this way: *"I plead with you
to give your bodies to God. Let them be a living and holy
sacrifice — the kind he will accept. When you think of
what he has done for you, is this too much to ask?"*[3] Most

of the time, we attempt to set our own life purpose. But we didn't create our life, so this doesn't always work well. Sometimes we live frustrated lives with little or no meaning or purpose. God created us, and He intends for us to grow and develop in areas we may have never considered. We will never know the possibilities that await us until we take Him up on His offer to guide us.

Regardless of who you are, God is serious about your life. Jesus is searching for people who will follow Him so that He can involve them in His eternal plan. Jesus said, *"All of us must quickly carry out the task assigned to us by the one who sent me."*[4] But you cannot carry out your life purpose until you decide to accept His plan for your life and Him as your Savior. Only then can you understand and summarize *God's purpose* for your life.

Summarize God's Purpose For You

Determine to take an action step: Write down a short statement of what you believe God's purpose is for your life. Even if you don't get it right at first, you are in the top 6% of Americans just because you have created a life purpose statement. Most people never take the time to establish this type of statement for their lives. Determine to make it a working statement; allow this to be a dynamic process, one that will be changed and adjusted as you grow and develop.

When you begin to consider God's purpose for your life, you may discover other related issues. Writing down your statement will force you to think about the direction your life is taking. It will also compel you to sort through what you value and hold most important. When you create a personal purpose statement, you also determine who or what will be the center of your life. This gives direction to your career, your finances, your family and just about everything else that matters to you.

Actually, whatever is at the center of your life is your god. All of our lives are centered on something—success, our spouse, money, ourselves—but is it the *best* center for our lives? The Bible says, *"Delight in the Lord, and he will give you the desires of your heart."* [5] God wants to be the center of your life!

How do you know when God is at the center of your life? When He is the center, you automatically align yourself to His way of operating and thinking. This has traditionally been called "worship." When God is not the center of our life, we worry. Worry is an indicator of a life out of alignment with God and His ways. As soon as we let God resume His rightful place at the center of our life, we will experience a quiet, calming peace, "not a peace as the world gives." [6] This new perspective will give purpose and hope. When you think about it, living on purpose is the only way to really live.

Take the time to pause at the close of this chapter and write a detailed life purpose statement. It is also helpful to summarize it into a brief repeatable phrase that you can use to guide and inspire you on a daily basis. When we remind ourselves daily that we are on a mission for the God of the universe, it will change our way of operating.

I have pared my life statement down to the sentence, *I want to live as a fully devoted follower of Christ, and allow this to influence me as a Christ-centered husband and father, to become more like Jesus in my actions, thoughts and dealings.* It's long, but it covers it all for me. Because it's all there in one sentence, I can use it as a reference point for my life. When I tend to venture off course, I can correct it based on what I have determined to be most important to me.

THINKING ABOUT IT

Something to Chew On:

What confusion do I have when it comes to sorting out my life purpose?

Verse to Remember:

"For David... served the purpose of God in his own generation." Acts 13:36, NASB

Point to Ponder:

Is living with purpose the best way for me to live?

My Life Purpose Statement:

IF GOD WOULD GRANT ME JUST ONE WISH, WHAT WOULD I ASK FOR?

"And now these three remain: faith, hope and love. But the greatest of these is love."

1 Corinthians 13:13

Like the characters in the fabled story of Aladdin's lamp, most of us would love to ask an all-powerful being to grant our fondest wishes. I asked this question to a group of friends one day, and it sparked quite a discussion. The first thought that came to most of our minds was about money. "Why not ask for a million dollars?" one said. "Why not a billion?" said another. "How about an incredible house with all the trimmings: pool, boats, cars, a jet with an airfield out back, maids and gardeners, the works?" "For that matter, why not an island?"

Then our thoughts shifted from a wealthy life to an impressive life. "Maybe we should ask for athletic ability to make it into a sports hall of fame?" "How about leadership skills that would net a CEO position in a Fortune 500 company?" "As long as we're dreaming, why not wish for the brains and prowess to earn a Nobel Prize?"

So what about you? If you could ask God for any one thing, what would it be?

One Thing

The problem with wealth is that it can't buy happiness.
Read up on what happens to those who win the lottery;
most of them lose their money,
their marriage or their zest for
life within a few years of win-
ning. Fame and achievement
don't last either. I have a dis-
tant relative who's in the NFL Hall of Fame; he's also in
a rest home with few visitors.

*"When you wish upon a star
Makes no difference who you ar
Anything your heart desires
Will come to you."* Jiminy Cricket

Most of our wishes are only skin-deep; they tend
to center on a change in *circumstances*. The key to lasting fulfillment is a change in *character*, which is why the
happiest people you know usually aren't the wealthiest or
most famous. They're the ones who've learned to love their
life and the people around them. But changes in character don't happen with the nod of a head or the clapping of
hands. The process of maturing takes a lifetime of right
thinking, right attitude and good decisions.

The Most Important Thing

One time, a Jewish scholar asked Jesus, "What is the
most important commandment?" Jesus' answer was
simple: love. "Love the Lord and love people," He said.[7]
I suggest that if you could only have one wish granted,
this would be the one—not that people would love you,
but that you would truly love people. Loving God and
people is the not-so-secret formula for a life of fulfillment and significance. The Apostle Paul wrote the book
of Philippians from prison, he was chained to a guard
24 hours a day, and yet he said, "I rejoice."[8] Philippians
is the most joyful book in the New Testament because,
even though locked away, Paul was loving the people
who were chained to him.

Some people think that God has a hidden agenda behind His commandments. They suspect He told us not to lie, steal or covet our neighbor's wife because His narrow morals are offended by it. But in reality, God designated certain actions off-limits because He knew indulging in them would hurt us, not Him. So you should stay away from the things God says are sinful because they'll harm you! God loves you with no hidden agenda. He shoots straight, because He wants your life to go well. He never takes pleasure in your pain, mistakes or suffering—only in your success, progress and contributions to the betterment of the world.

And God not only loves us enough to suggest we stay away from things He knows will harm us; He clearly explains what we should steer toward so that our lives will improve on a deep and permanent (you could even say, "eternal") basis. So, when a curious scholar wants to know the most important things to do, Jesus says, "That's easy: Love God and love people." Love God, and you will experience life not only in its optimum natural and supernatural state. Love people, and you will find yourself fulfilled in ways you never imagined as you watch the objects of your love succeed. Watch any parent watching their infant take his first steps or their preschooler scoring her first goal, and you'll see joy unbounded. Ask any parent what is richer: succeeding themselves, or seeing their child succeed. You'll find that for one who loves, personal success only comes from helping others succeed.

A Picture of Love

At no time in history was there a better picture of love than Jesus dying on the Cross. In the midst of His agonizing torment, the Savior looked down on His tormenters and whispered, "Father, forgive them, for they don't know what they are doing." [9] These words weren't begrudgingly forced from Jesus' lips; He said them because they were the sentiment of His heart. As He looked down on those who were causing Him pain, instead of feeling hatred or anger, He felt love. Because Jesus had lived His entire life around the commandment to love God and love people, in His worst moment His thoughts were still about others and how God might be merciful to them.

If I could ask for just one thing, it would be that I would truly and purely love God and love people. Those who have done this well are the people I admire most in life. People like St. Francis of Assisi, Billy Graham, Susanna Wesley[10] and Mother Teresa have a certain untouchability to them; their suffering never seemed to damage them. It was diffused by their focus on others. When you care about others, you care less and less about yourself, so that even if you decrease in status or stature (or increase in pain and challenge), as long as others around you are increasing or flourishing, you feel joy and pleasure. This is the very essence of who God is; He is all about others. For the truly loving person, true pain only occurs when those they love get hurt or do hurtful things. So God is very concerned about our behavior, because He is *very* concerned for us.

THINKING ABOUT IT

Something to Chew On:

When love is your driving purpose and ultimate goal, there isn't anything that can keep you from achieving it.

Verse to Remember:

Jesus replied, *"Love the Lord your God with all your heart and with all your soul and with all your mind. This is the first and greatest commandment. And the second is like it: 'Love your neighbor as yourself.'"* Matthew 22:37-38

Point to Ponder:

Is it really true that loving God and people is the not-so-secret formula for a life of fulfillment and significance?

My Thoughts on the Subject:

_____

_____

_____

_____

_____

_____

HOW DO I CHANGE MY BEHAVIOR?

*"God said, 'I will live with them
and walk with them, and I will be their God,
and they will be my people'. "*

2 Corinthians 6:16-17

From my home near the California coast, I can regularly see a cluster of hot-air balloons. Before a balloon
is launched, the ground is covered with a limp, color-
ful canvas that begins to ripple and take form when the
burner is fired up. The hot air slowly fills the cloth. Before long, the air lifts the balloon off the ground, where
it hovers ready for flight until its earthbound tether is
released. Soon, all can enjoy the beautiful sight of ex-
ploding colors as many balloons hang in the sky.

Much like those hot-air balloons, individuals who
are pursuing God remain earthbound until their tethers
are no longer grounded. Just as the rope holding the
balloon must be released or cut, so too must one cut
his/her ties with earth, so that the "God experience" is
not simply another item on one's to-do list.

If we spend our lives pursuing the answers to
spiritual questions, there will come a time in which we
realize that the answers alone will not leave a lasting
satisfaction. Metaphorically speaking, finding answers

to our questions will not make us airborne. It takes something far more powerful than a piece of missing information; we must find something that will produce lasting life change. A critical step to living the life of a Christ-follower is to receive the power of God through the Holy Spirit.

The Bible tells us that God has shown Himself to us in three ways: God the Father, God the Son and God the Holy Spirit, collectively referred to as the "Godhead." One early Christian leader described the three entities

"To never improve and change is to miss the point of living."
Albert Einstein

of the Godhead to be like water. Water that is placed in a freezer becomes a solid; it is hard and firm. Ice best illustrates God the Father, who is solid, immovable, holds the universe together and provides order. Water poured into a glass will take the shape of the glass, just as God the Son took the shape of a human body and became one of us. Finally, God the Holy Spirit is as water placed in a heating teapot. Before long, the steam shoots across the room and gently lands upon everything in its realm. The steam cannot be traced or located. God has planned for the Holy Spirit to be the agent of change for Christ-followers, and our behavior changes when the Holy Spirit dwells within us.

When I was 25 years old, I became a pastor of a small, rural church. During that first year, I was befriended by a member named Jim, who was a church leader and the town doctor. One day, Jim put his arm around me and said, "I really like you, but you are going to get disillusioned and be disappointed." Puzzled, I asked Jim what he meant, and he said, "You really believe that people will change. People seldom ever change. They keep on making the same mistakes. Liars keep on lying, greedy people stay greedy and adulterers keep on committing adultery. I just hate to see you have your bubble burst."

When I think about what Jim said, I must agree with him. Apart from the transforming power of Christ, we are unable to change. Perhaps you have previously attempted to make behavioral changes but felt helpless and unable to make those changes last. Without the Holy Spirit within us, we are unable to truly modify our behavior. Now, the question is not "Will I change my behavior?" but rather "Will I allow the Holy Spirit of God to change my behavior?"

Over the course of this study, we have investigated the claims of Christ, authority of Scripture and the nature of God. Now we must embrace God in all His forms. If you have been drawn to trust God, I hope that you respond to the growing revelation of who He Is. When we embrace Him, He gives our lives a new motivation and purpose. As the Father, Son and Holy Spirit, He has an impact on us and changes our behavior.

The amazing truth that comes from the Bible is that God the Father has provided a way for each of us to change and receive a new life. The Bible tells us, *"We are God's workmanship created in Christ Jesus to do good works."*[11] Again, God does not simply extend this plan as a casual take-it-or-leave-it affair; He expects us to fully embrace this mission.

The apostle and Biblical writer Paul says, *"I plead with you to give your bodies to God. Let them be a living and holy sacrifice—the kind he will accept. When you think of what he has done for you, is this too much to ask... let God transform you into a new person by changing the way you think. Then you will know what God wants you to do and you will know how good and pleasing and perfect his will really is."*[12]

This verse reminds us that God desires to change and transform us into His plan and purpose for us. Paul is begging us to use this life to glorify God. Paul knows the fleeting nature of our lives on earth. In addition, he realizes that the greatest tragedy in life is not death, but a life that is lived without reflecting the likeness of the Father. Our behavior can only change when we allow God the Holy Spirit to do the transforming work in us.

THINKING ABOUT IT

Something to Chew On:

Now that you have explored *The God Questions*, you have the opportunity to take another step toward God. This step requires that we make necessary life adjustments and changes to accommodate our new understanding of God.

Verse to Remember:

"But the word of the Lord stands forever." 1 Peter 1:25

Point to Ponder:

Will I continue to take the necessary steps to embrace the Holy Spirit of God for the necessary life changes that await me?

My Thoughts on the Subject:

_____

_____

_____

_____

_____

_____

_____

WHAT DOES 'LOVING GOD AND LOVING PEOPLE' LOOK LIKE?

"God ...is able to do immeasurably more than all we ask or imagine, according to his power that is at work within us."

Ephesians 3:20

God Wants Us to Live by Priorities, Not Pressures

In our busy lives, it is easy to lose sight of the purpose for which we were created: To love God, to know Him and to bring Him glory. *"Love the LORD your God with all your heart, with all your soul, and with all your strength."* [13]

From the earliest days, God wanted to remind us that we need to monitor our priorities. The Bible says that humans were made to respond to God. Yet, the many choices and distractions we have in life make it difficult to live according to the priorities set forth by God. Sometimes it is much easier to fill our days responding to problems and pressures.

I recently composed my "life plan" with the assistance of a coach who helped me sort through the various priorities and distractions of my life. We went through a thorough charting and evaluation process. In the end, the priorities that I chose to build my life around were very basic—and were laid out in the Bible. I found my priorities to be first, to live a Christ-centered life; second, to grow as a person by using my spiritual gifts to make a difference in our world; and third, to honor God with my marriage and family. I found that it is one thing to recognize the top three priorities in my life, but quite another to make the life-adjustments necessary to execute those priorities. Living by priorities requires deliberate intention and choice.

As I was working on my own life plan, I was reminded that, as a Christ-follower, my top priorities should be aligned to the ones that the Scripture calls us to live by. When we do, we find that He has a plan for us to prosper and flourish. One could say that God has planned for us to live three-dimensionally. Jesus proclaimed this relational priority, which is divided into the dimensions of loving God, loving self and loving others. In the New Testament, there is a passage called the *Shema*. It is designed to prompt us to adjust our attitude toward Christ and others. It instructs us to *"love God with all your heart, with all your understanding and with all your strength, and to love your neighbor as yourself. There is no commandment greater than these."* [14] This is central to everything that we do, so it's important to get it right.

> *"The actions we take will always express our priorities."*
>
> Mohandas Gandhi

Love and Know God

We were made to know and relate to God. We were made to live in close relationship with Him. This drives and influences all of our other relationships. It also sets the tone for how we live our lives.

Love Yourself and Develop a Plan for Personal Growth and Maturity

Loving ourselves is not a hedonistic action. When we are in balance relationally (God first, ourselves second) we will not be acting selfishly or in the self-serving manner encouraged by our culture. A healthy "self-love" should be an outgrowth of how we love God the Father. When we love ourselves the way that God loves us, we will not venture into inappropriate pursuits; rather, we will live for the purposes for which God has specifically crafted us, and this life is fulfilling.

Care for and Love Others, Especially Your Family

Finally, we are told to love others as an outgrowth of how God loves us. This dimension reflects a healthy view of God's love that is practically demonstrated toward others.

The Bible tells us *"that we are God's workmanship, created in Christ Jesus to do good works which God prepared in advance that we should do."* [15] It is both humbling and exciting to realize that God the Father has a special mission and purpose for each one of us. He has a plan that takes into consideration our unique talents and gifts.

When you release your life to Christ, you come under new ownership. God places His mission on you, and He will replace your worries and anxieties about fulfilling your mission with a newfound confidence in Him. Jesus said, *"Seek first his kingdom and his righteousness, and all these things will be given to you as well... do not worry about tomorrow... each day has enough trouble of its own."* [16]

God is most interested in developing our character and relationships because, in doing so, His purpose is fulfilled. As a result, there will be evidence of His work in our life. *"It is called the fruit of the Spirit. These are love, joy, peace, patience, kindness, goodness, faithfulness, gentleness and self-control."* [17]

Beyond the spiritual development plan that God has for you, He also offers to guide and direct your life. He wants to help you with your focus and decision-making. What matters most is that you fulfill God's eternal purpose for your life, regardless of where you live or work or whom you may marry. Decisions regarding God's will for your job, marriage and material and geographical lifestyle are important, but they are secondary to His overall purpose for you. You have been given a new commission, which is to live not for yourself, but rather for an audience of One—to live for God.

You may be feeling a little overwhelmed with all this information. It may be astounding that the God of the universe wants to develop you. You may even question how He could or why He cares that much for you, and it may be perplexing that He desires to develop spiritual qualities in you.

If you are just beginning your Christian walk, I would encourage you to begin reading the gospel portion of the New Testament. A good book to begin with is the Gospel of John. John is an easily understandable introduction to the life of Christ. Follow John with Ephesians, and then proceed to any of the books that are Paul's letters to the cities, such as Colossians, Thessalonians, Galatians, Philippians and/or Romans. This journey is an awesome adventure. I hope and pray that you discover the amazing truths of God's deep love and care for you.

THINKING ABOUT IT

Something to Chew On:

How has God spoken to you to adjust your priorities? How do you think that God's revelation in the Bible will impact this adjustment of priorities?

Verse to Remember:

"But seek first his kingdom and his righteousness, and all these things will be given to you as well." Matthew 6:33

Point to Ponder:

God desires to reveal to me His plan for my life.

My Thoughts on the Subject:

_____

_____

_____

_____

_____

_____

_____

HOW DO I GET STARTED?

---

*"Much is required from those to whom much is
given, and much more is required from those
to whom much more is given."*

Luke 12:48, NLT

As you come to the close of a learning experience, you
can respond in one of two ways. Some people say, "Well,
the adventure is over. Now I'm going to start a new
chapter. I wonder where I'll go with it." Others have a
different response: "The adventure is just beginning.
Now that I know what I know, God can use me in bold
new ways." I hope you'll choose the bold way.

The truth is, a whole new world stands before you.
What you've learned in the last 40 days has put you
ahead of many others in your understanding of God. In
the last six weeks, we've covered more great answers
than many seminaries and Bible college students do in
a full semester. But what if you forget the answers we've
covered? They're right here for you to pick up, review
and share with friends.

Here are six suggestions for the first steps in your
bold new adventure:

Receive Christ

Today can be your day of salvation. The Bible says, *"To
all who received him, to those who believed in his name,*

he gave the right to become children of God..."[18] If you haven't already done so, pray this prayer right now: "Lord Jesus, I believe in You. I receive You now into my life. I want to be a Christian. Forgive me for the things I have done wrong. Lead me from now on." If you've prayed that prayer, all the promises of God and all the truths of this book will be applied to your life—starting right now! The Bible says, *"There is rejoicing in the presence of the angels of God over one sinner who repents."*[19]

Recognize the Gift You've Been Given

We live in an information-rich society. You've learned much in these last 40 days, and with that knowledge comes responsibility. Jesus said, *"Much is required from those to whom much is given, and much more is required from those to whom much more is given."*[20]

Share What You've Learned

The Apostle Paul told his friends, *"Teach these great truths to trustworthy people who are able to pass them on to others."*[21] You've got some great answers that friends and loved ones need to hear. You don't have to be pushy; in fact, pushiness usually just pushes people away. Ask permission to share what you've learned, and then sensitively begin a dialogue about these truths.

Look for Opportunities

God knows that you now have some really good answers to really good questions. As an "available" information source, don't be surprised if sincere, seeking people find their way to you. Who knows, maybe as soon as this afternoon or tomorrow morning God will nudge someone your way! Just remember though: No one was ever argued into heaven. Offer answers politely; don't force yourself on people. God says, *"If you are asked about your Christian hope, always be ready to explain it. But you must do this in a gentle and respectful way."* [22]

Pray for Opportunities

Paul said, *"And pray for us, too, that God may open a door for our message, so that we may proclaim the mystery of Christ..."* [23]

Give the Gift of Answers

If you find friends who have questions, loan them your book. Better still, give them their own copy and offer to walk through the adventure with them.

2 Kings 6-7 records a gripping story about a siege that took place in the city of Samaria during the 9th century, B.C. The Syrian army was so effective in shutting off supplies to the city that people were starving to death. In desperation, the Samaritans resorted to cannibalism. [24] One night, a rumor circulated in the Syrian army camp: a superior force of Egyptian soldiers was about to arrive and overwhelm them. In a mass panic, the Syrians fled without even breaking camp. Under cover of darkness, they left their tents, their plunder and huge stores of food behind.

"Now, who will want to harm you if you are eager to do good? But even if you suffer for doing what is right, God will reward you for it. So don't be afraid and don't worry. Instead, you must worship Christ as Lord of your life. And if you are asked about your Christian hope, always be ready to explain it. But you must do this in a gentle and respectful way."
1 Peter 3:13-16, NLT

Meanwhile, four starving Samaritans decided to sneak out of the city and surrender to the Syrians. As they reached the edge of the Syrian camp, they realized they had struck the Mother Lode! They gorged themselves and then began collecting as much booty as they could carry, hiding it in nearby caves for future retrieval. Suddenly it struck them: not far away was a city full of starving people they loved who had no idea of the treasures within their reach. The foursome said to each other, "We're not doing right. This is a day of good news and we are keeping it to ourselves." [25] With joyful resolve, they headed back to the city to share the good news with the rest of the citizens. Imagine how grateful those citizens were when, just a few hours later, they got to sample the goods for themselves. If *The God Questions* has enriched you in any way, you might consider sharing it with people you love.

Keep Your Fork

I don't know whether this story is true or not, but I love the point it makes:

An elderly woman was diagnosed with a terminal illness and given three months to live. She invited her pastor over to help with final preparations. The pastor took copious notes and prayed with her. As he was turning to leave, he asked, "Is there anything else I can do for you?"

"Yes," she said, "There is one more thing. I want you to bury me with a fork in my hand."

As the pastor smiled, a wrinkle of confusion appeared on his brow. The woman explained, "Over the years I have been to hundreds of church socials and pot-luck dinners. When the main course is cleared, someone always leans over and says, 'Keep your fork.' That's my favorite part of the evening because it means something better is coming, like chocolate cake or apple pie. So, I'm hoping that as people look at me there in the casket with a fork in my hand, they'll wonder, 'What's with the fork?' At the end of the service I want you to tell them, 'Keep your fork, because the best is yet to come!'" [26]

THINKING ABOUT IT

Something to Chew On:

No society in history has had as much accessible information as we do. The problem isn't finding a tree that holds knowledge; the problem is finding the tree that holds the knowledge *you need*. Rejoice in the new knowledge you've collected during this study!

Verse to Remember:

"If you are asked about your Christian hope, always be ready to explain it. But you must do this in a gentle and respectful way." 1 Peter 3:15, NLT

Point to Ponder:

What is the single most important thing I learned from this adventure? (Write it down.) What am I going to do with what I've learned?

My Thoughts on the Subject:

END NOTES

WHAT'S THE PURPOSE OF MY LIFE?
1. Psalm 139:16, LB.
2. Ephesians 2:10.
3. Romans 12:1.
4. John 9:4.
5. Psalm 37:4.
6. John 14:27.

If GOD WOULD GRANT ME JUST ONE WISH, WHAT WOULD I ASK FOR?
7. Matthew 22:36-37.
8. Philippians 1:18.
9. Luke 23:34.
10. Susanna Wesley was a 17th century pastor's wife and the mother of Jonathan and Charles Wesley, as well as 15 other children. Her life was riveted on loving her children, her church and the people of her village.

HOW DO I CHANGE MY BEHAVIOR?
11. Ephesians 2:10.
12. Romans 12:1-5.

WHAT DOES 'LOVING GOD AND LOVING PEOPLE' LOOK LIKE?
13. Mark 12:30.
14. Mark 12:30-31.
15. Ephesians 2:10.
16. Matthew 6:33-34.
17. Galatians 5:22.

HOW DO I GET STARTED?
18. John 1:12.
19. Luke 15:16.
20. Luke 12:38b.
21. 2 Timothy 2:2, NLT.
22. 1 Peter 3:15, NLT.
23. Colossians 4:3.
24. 2 Kings 6:28-29.
25. 2 Kings 7:9.
26. A retelling of a short story by Roger William Thomas.

Small Group Study Guide

INTRODUCTION

They spent their time learning the Apostles'
teaching, sharing, breaking bread,
and praying together.

Acts 2:42

Why Small Groups?

Significant things happen in community. People in our culture tend to be individualists. When we work in community, God shows up in a new and different way.

Did you know that geese fly farther than eagles? Geese can travel a span of up to 4,000 miles, but an eagle seldom ventures more than 160 miles from its birthplace.

"I remember one day as a young boy, lying on my back staring up at the sky, watching the geese migrate. It was such a sight to see them fly 1,000 feet or more above me. As I watched, the lead goose suddenly veered out of formation and started heading to the back of the pack. A bird that had been flying in second place moved up to fill the vacated lead position. I had just witnessed the amazing benefits of being in community."[1]

The young boy in the story witnessed a behavior in wild geese commonly referred to as "drafting." The head goose cuts the air with his wings, making the travel easier for the whole flock. The effort required to be the lead windbreaker is exhausting, so they take turns leading the flock. The lead bird will fly an average of a hundred miles before relinquishing his position to the next bird in the formation. God designed geese—and people—to perform most effectively as a team.

Although God designed us to function like geese, we often prefer to travel solo, like an eagle. Most of us see ourselves as solitary, self-sufficient, strong individuals. We cover our weaknesses and avoid being known. But just as an eagle becomes fatigued when it must absorb all of the effort of flying by itself, life has a way of creating weariness. And just like these geese depend on each other, we hope you will also help each other along in this quest to answer *The God Questions*.

Christians often have as many "God Questions" as do spiritual explorers. Christians decide to move forward in their faith despite these questions, but some spiritual explorers allow the questions to become a hindrance to further advancement. This Study Guide is designed to help you reach unchurched seekers who have serious questions about the Christian faith. The people in your small group may have a wide variety of backgrounds and experiences. If you are a small group leader, help your group find a measure of common ground that will move you all forward together.

If this is your first experience in leading a small group, prayerfully ask the Lord to help you find the right individuals and to invite them to join you. This study is designed to accommodate almost anyone, seeker or believer. So open up your group to people from all walks of life, and have fun as you seek the truth as a community!

How to Start a Discussion Group

Pray about whom to invite to the group. All of us have friends who ask hard questions. This study is designed to help you start spiritual conversations with such people. Don't worry that the group will raise questions that you don't know how to answer. You are only responsible for developing an environment that encourages honest and open dialogue.

Feel Free to Keep the Group Small. Don't worry about getting commitments from a large number of people. Sometimes the best groups are small gatherings around a table. People are more willing to share when in smaller groups as opposed to large ones. If a large group arrives, divide it into smaller subgroups to answer the discussion questions. Consider dividing groups by gender for a more focused and relevant perspective.

Be relaxed and friendly. Make sure you greet the people at the door with a smile. This will set the mood for the very first meeting. Remember that the people who are coming to your group are taking a big risk; it can be scary to attend a small group or visit someone's home for the first time. Give a warm welcome, and assure group members that their contributions are important.

Help guide them through the course. Be sure that everyone has read that week's chapters. Remind them that their discussion and participation will be enhanced when they fully engage in the overall program.

Do everything you can to help the group bond. The main benefit of leading a small group is not the learning—it's the sharing. People will only share if they know you care. At your first meeting, get everyone's name, e-mail and phone number. During the following weeks, be sure to call people who were absent, but not as a police officer; let them know they were missed. Try passing a note card around and have everyone jot a quick sentence encouraging absentees to come back the next time the group meets. Consider sending an e-mail each week to touch base with the group and reiterate prayer requests.

Choose a co-leader for the group. Don't try to care for everyone all by yourself. Consider the gifting of the people in your group and choose someone to help you lead, or ask someone you trust to join the group as a leader with you.

Don't be afraid to ask the group to make a commitment. Explain that this group will be meeting for the next six weeks, and ask each member to commit to attending every meeting. Explain that their consistency is important to bonding the group, and every unique perspective is valuable. Encourage them to also participate in the weekend services at your church, so that a connection can be established with a larger church body.

Tips for New Leaders

Remember you're not alone. God loves these people, and He loves you. In calling you to lead this group, God desires to love these people through you. Trust Him to provide everything you'll need to accomplish His will for these people, including resources, patience, stamina, ideas and more.

Pray regularly for everyone in the group by name. Ask God to speak to each attendee directly and personally, and ask Him to give you the words and direction that will bring people to Him. Ask Him to give you discernment to see what the group needs and what delivery would best reach them.

Just be yourself. Your authenticity is the most unique, valuable quality you bring to this group. It's OK to admit when you don't have the answer to a question. Apologize when you make a mistake. Research answers together with your group; these moments can be the best learning opportunities that your group will experience.

Prepare for the meeting ahead of time. Study the material beforehand; the perspective and insights you discover will help the group as they work through the material.

Be patient when you ask a question. Small group leaders can be uncomfortable when no one speaks. During this "dead-air," it's tempting for the group leader to rush in and answer the question. Fight this urge. If you continue to talk, everyone else will be an observer. Be patient and give people time to form an answer. New groups require some long pauses, but God works in them to move people to respond.

Provide transitions between questions. You can ask if anyone would like to read a paragraph or Bible passage; this allows people to participate without having to risk giving a wrong answer. You may ask people directly to read a passage or answer a question, but don't insist. Be sure to thank the person when they participate.

Guidelines for Small Group Members

Share these guidelines with your group to maximize the benefit of their time together.

Maintain confidentiality. Remember that everything shared in your small group is to be considered confidential. This protects the group's status as a safe, supportive, accepting place for its members. Unless you've been given expressed permission, do not share anything from your discussion outside your small group.

Be authentic. Do your best to be open and honest during discussions. Your transparency will encourage others to do the same.

Respect one another. Remember that every person has the right to his/her opinion. All questions are encouraged and respected. Listen attentively to others without interrupting. Be slow to judge one another. Be careful of using sentences beginning with, "You should..." or "You ought..." Do not give advice that is not specifically solicited.

Prioritize this group. Give the group meetings priority in your schedule, and if you are unable to attend or will be late to a meeting, contact the group leader.

Be prepared. Read the lesson each week before you arrive at the group meeting, and come ready to share.

Participate. Participate in the discussion, but be brief enough to allow others to share as well.

Provide feedback. Feel free to offer suggestions and encouragement to the group leader at any time during the study.

Provide support to one another. Actively support the mission and values of the study and follow the directions given by your leader. Refrain from gossip or criticism. If you have concerns about a member's views or statements, communicate directly and appropriately with that person. Group members are given permission to call one another when support or prayer is needed.

CAN GOD REALLY ANSWER MY QUESTIONS?

Note: This study is intended as an introductory session to the book, The God Questions. The questions in this session will start your group thinking about God Questions. This session is meant to precede Week One in The God Questions book.

OPEN IN PRAYER

CONNECT TOGETHER

Icebreaker Question: If you could ask God any one question and you knew He would answer, what would it be? Why?

DISCUSS TOGETHER

READ PROVERBS 1:7 AND 9:10.

Now, read the definition of "Reverential Fear," below.

> *Reverential fear of the Lord is the prerequisite of knowledge. The term yir'ah can describe dread (Dt. 1:29), being terrified (Jonah 1:10), standing in awe (1 Kings 3:28), or having reverence (Lev. 19:3). With the Lord as the object, yir'ah captures both aspects of shrinking back in fear and of drawing close in awe. It is not a trembling dread that paralyzes action, but neither is it a polite reverence.*[2]

QUESTION 1: What do you think Proverbs 1:7 means when it says, "The fear of the Lord is the beginning of wisdom"? How does wisdom begin with fear of God?

QUESTION 2: Proverbs 9:10 says something similar, but slightly different. What is the difference between wisdom and knowledge? Why must they both start with God?

QUESTION 3: The second half of Proverbs 9:10 says, "Knowledge of the Holy One is understanding." What do you think that means?

QUESTION 4: The first week's readings in *The God Questions* answer questions about God's existence and nature. What difference does it make whether God exists or not? And does it really matter whether He is weak or strong, caring or indifferent, all-knowing or unaware?

READ 1 THESSALONIANS 5:21.

QUESTION 5: This verse gives you permission to seek answers to difficult questions and expect rational answers. What does it look like to "test everything"? What's your reaction to this verse?

QUESTION 6: The study you are about to begin will use five truth sources—history, science, logic, archaeology and the Bible—to help you "search out" matters about God. Rank them in order from most important (or reliable, or authoritative) to least important and explain why you put them in that order.

_____

_____

_____

_____

QUESTION 7: Mark Twain once said, "It isn't the parts of the Bible I can't understand that bother me; it is the parts that I do understand." Which is more troubling to you, the parts you understand or the parts you don't?

_____

_____

_____

QUESTION 8: As we begin this study, what do you hope to get out of it?

_____

_____

_____

_____

GOD QUESTIONS CHALLENGE FOR THE WEEK

Choose someone from your circle of relationships (family, friends, neighbors, work associates, acquaintances) with whom you can share what you are learning as you investigate *The God Questions*. Tell the group who that person is (if you feel comfortable) and how you will be praying for him or her this week.

SHARE TOGETHER

Have each member of your group share a prayer request. Write down each person's request and commit to praying for one another throughout the week.

CLOSE IN PRAYER

IS GOD REAL?

OPEN IN PRAYER

CONNECT TOGETHER

ICEBREAKER QUESTION: Select one of the icebreaker questions below and share your answer with your group.

- What is your favorite memory of a time when you were outdoors?
- What makes you think about God most when you are in nature?

DISCUSS TOGETHER

READ PSALM 19:1-2.

QUESTION 1: Has Nature ever taught you something about God? Think of a time when you observed something about Nature that affected your view of God. Share the story with your group. What did you learn about God from that experience?

QUESTION 2: In what ways does the night sky "display knowledge" that's relevant to whether or not God is real?

QUESTION 3: Write down five or six adjectives you would use to describe the earth, plants and animals as a whole creation. As you look at that list of adjectives, what can be known about God from what He has created?

READ ECCLESIASTES 3:11.

QUESTION 4: According to this verse, in what ways has God made humans aware of eternity? How do we respond to the idea of eternity differently than other living creatures? Give some examples.

QUESTION 5: How does our limited perspective affect our understanding of God and His creation? Give an example of something you've wondered about the universe (e.g., its physical properties, or the characteristics of plants, animals or people).

_____

_____

_____

_____

-READ ROMANS 1:19-20.

QUESTION 6: How do these verses compare with Psalm 19:1-2? What do they say that's similar? What do they add to our understanding of how God is known?

_____

_____

_____

_____

QUESTION 7: If you were God, what way or ways do you think you would use to reveal yourself to people?

_____

_____

_____

_____

QUESTION 8: How has God revealed Himself to you?

_____

_____

_____

_____

GOD QUESTIONS CHALLENGE FOR THE WEEK

Begin a personal "God sightings" record, below. As a group, come up with one example for each of the two sections. Then, on your own, try to write down other examples in one or both sections every day this week.

Things that point to God's existence:

_____

_____

Ways I have experienced God:

_____

_____

QUESTION 9: How would you like to have God reveal Himself to you?

_____

_____

_____

_____

SHARE TOGETHER

Have each member of your group share a prayer request. (You might want to use your response to Question 9 as your prayer request.) Write down each person's request and commit to praying for one another throughout the week.

CLOSE IN PRAYER

IS THE BIBLE TRUE?

OPEN IN PRAYER

CONNECT TOGETHER

ICEBREAKER QUESTION: What is your favorite Bible story or verse? Why do you like that particular one?

DISCUSS TOGETHER

READ PROVERBS 30:5, PSALM 12:6 AND PSALM 19:7.

QUESTION 1: The Bible repeatedly says that God's Word is flawless and perfect. How important is it to you that the Bible is flawless? Why?

QUESTION 2: As you read through Day 8 and Day 9 in Week Two, was there anything about the Bible's authorship or history that particularly impressed you, or even surprised you? What stood out and why?

_____

_____

_____

_____

QUESTION 3: Do you agree or disagree with the following statement: Most people, deep down inside, believe that the Bible is true.

_____

_____

_____

_____

QUESTION 4: What reasons do you think people have for doubting the accuracy or authenticity of the Bible?

_____

_____

_____

_____

QUESTION 5: The study for Day 11 listed evidence for the Bible from science, archaeology and prophecy. Pick one or two points that made the biggest impression on you and share your thoughts with your group.

_____

_____

_____

_____

READ 2 TIMOTHY 3:16.

QUESTION 6: What phrase is used in this verse to describe Scripture? How would it impact your reliance on the Bible if it were simply wisdom from men rather than inspired by God?

---

*READ PSALM 119:35, PROVERBS 3:5-6,
PROVERBS 14:12 AND PSALM 119:105.*

QUESTION 7: What do these verses mean when they refer to a path or a way? How should God's Word affect our decision-making? What's the likely outcome when we use our own wisdom versus when we rely on the Bible?

QUESTION 8: Has what you've learned about the Bible this week changed your thinking or strengthened your convictions about its authority in your life? How do you want to live differently as a result of this week's study?

GOD QUESTIONS CHALLENGE FOR THE WEEK

Pick a book of the Bible and then do a little research on that book—when it was written, who wrote it and the author's purpose in writing. You can find some of this information by using a study Bible, a Bible encyclopedia or an online resource site like BibleGateway.com.

_____

_____

_____

_____

_____

_____

SHARE TOGETHER

Have each member of your group share a prayer request. Write down each person's request and commit to praying for one another throughout the week.

CLOSE IN PRAYER

DO ALL ROADS LEAD TO HEAVEN?

OPEN IN PRAYER

CONNECT TOGETHER

ICEBREAKER QUESTION: Who was your first friend from a different ethnic or cultural background? What did you learn from your friend about his/her culture and upbringing?

DISCUSS TOGETHER

READ JOHN 14:6.

QUESTION 1: What are some widely accepted "truths" that you question or believe to be false?

QUESTION 2: Read through the list below. Which of these factors affect how you decide what is true? In the column labeled Me, put an X beside the ones that apply to you. Which of these do you believe affect how most other people decide what is true? Put an X beside those in the column labeled Others. Which of these methods seem the most unreliable?

ME	OTHERS
_____ What I read in the paper	_____ What they read in the paper
_____ What's accepted in my culture	_____ What's accepted in our culture
_____ What I learned in school	_____ What they learned in school
_____ What I see on TV or in movies	_____ What they see on TV or in movies
_____ What I was taught by my parents	_____ What they were taught by their parents
_____ What the Bible says	_____ What the Bible says
_____ Other _____	_____ Other _____

QUESTION 3: What words did Jesus intentionally use to describe Himself in John 14:6? How does this statement force us to make a decision about who Jesus is?

_____

_____

_____

_____

QUESTION 4: On a scale of 1 to 10, with 1 being the lowest and 10 the highest, rate the level at which Jesus' teachings affect your daily decisions. If you fully allowed Jesus to be "the way, the truth and the life" in your daily activities, how do you think your life would be different? What steps can you take to follow Jesus more closely?

1   2   3   4   5   6   7   8   9   10

READ JOHN 14:8-10, JOHN 8:54-58 AND MATTHEW 16:15-17.

QUESTION 5: One key difference between Christianity, Islam and a few other religions is the answer to the question, "Who is Jesus?" Based on these verses, who and what did Jesus claim to be?

_____

_____

_____

_____

QUESTION 6: Jesus taught that really knowing Him gives us knowledge of whom?

_____

_____

_____

_____

QUESTION 7: What does it mean to "know" someone? Give some practical examples of what it means to really know God. Name two to three things you can do to gain a better knowledge of God.

_____

_____

_____

_____

READ TITUS 3:5-6 AND EPHESIANS 2:8-9.

QUESTION 8: What difference does it make that God saves us out of His great mercy and not because of anything we do?

_____

_____

_____

_____

QUESTION 9: Why can't we boast in our salvation? How do these verses in Ephesians prompt you to act more humbly?

_____

_____

_____

_____

GOD QUESTIONS CHALLENGE FOR THE WEEK

Find one person you know who has a different religious view and gently engage them in a spiritual conversation. Ask them what they believe and why (i.e., what their religion teaches), and pray for an opportunity to also share what you know about Jesus and Christian beliefs.

Remember to be respectful as you talk with them. 1 Peter 3:15 teaches us to "always be prepared to give an answer to everyone who asks you to give the reason for the hope that you have. But do this with gentleness and respect." (NIV)

If you don't know anyone you can talk with, then pick one religion and either find a book in the library, or do an Internet search for more information on that religion. How do you see the concept of "grace versus works" illustrated in the contrast between this religion and Christianity?

SHARE TOGETHER

Have each member of your group share a prayer request. Write down each person's request and commit to praying for one another throughout the week.

CLOSE IN PRAYER

HOW CAN A GOOD GOD ALLOW SUFFERING?

OPEN IN PRAYER

CONNECT TOGETHER

ICEBREAKER QUESTION: What was the worst injury you've ever sustained? How did it happen, and how did you feel as you recovered from it?

DISCUSS TOGETHER

READ GENESIS 1:31 AND GENESIS 3:16-19.

Throughout Genesis 1, God evaluates each item He creates and pronounces them "good." The verses in Genesis 3 come after Adam and Eve have chosen to disobey God. In the Genesis 3 passage, God describes the consequences of what Adam and Eve have done.

QUESTION 1: Before Adam and Eve sinned, do you think evil existed in the world? What does this tell you about God's intention for His creation?

QUESTION 2: Review Genesis 3:16-19 and list two to three specific consequences of sin. Which of them stand out to you?

QUESTION 3: Give some present-day examples of how the consequences of sin affect our world.

READ ROMANS 8:20-22.

QUESTION 4: According to Romans 8, what portion of the world was affected by Adam and Eve's choice? Is the effect permanent?

READ JOHN 16:33, HEBREWS 4:14-16 AND

MATTHEW 11:28-30.

QUESTION 5: What do these Scriptures tell you about God's understanding of suffering and temptation? What does it mean to you to have God fully understand the struggles we face in this life? What's your emotional reaction to these verses?

_____

_____

_____

_____

QUESTION 6: How do these verses teach us to respond to suffering? What comfort do they offer?

_____

_____

_____

_____

READ ROMANS 5:3-5 AND JAMES 1:2-4.

QUESTION 7: In what ways do we learn and develop by going through the difficulties of life?

_____

_____

_____

_____

QUESTION 8: The reading for Day 24 includes a list of five ways in which God uses trials in a positive way. Think of a specific struggle you've had in the past three years. As you look through the list from Day 24, does that particular struggle fit with one of these five ways in which God works in our lives? Which one and why?

_____

_____

_____

_____

GOD QUESTIONS CHALLENGE FOR THE WEEK

Think and pray about your family and friends and choose someone you feel is going through a difficult time. In what way could you provide comfort and support to that friend or family member? It could be consistent prayer, time spent with them listening to their situation, or practical help and assistance with the problem. This week, commit to providing support to the person you've selected.

SHARE TOGETHER

Have each member of your group share a prayer request. Write down each person's request and commit to praying for one another throughout the week.

CLOSE IN PRAYER

WHAT'S THE PURPOSE OF THE CHURCH?

OPEN IN PRAYER

CONNECT TOGETHER

ICEBREAKER QUESTION: What was your experience with the church growing up? Did you attend one? If you did, what was it like?

DISCUSS TOGETHER

READ MATTHEW 16:13-20.

QUESTION 1: This announcement by Jesus takes place two years into His ministry. After the disciples have spent all this time with Him, Jesus quizzes them on who He is. When Peter correctly identifies Him as the Messiah ("the Christ"), Jesus tells them His purpose in coming. What is it?

QUESTION 2: The Christian church has founded or invented almost every major charity on earth, from hospitals to schools and universities to the YMCA, Salvation Army, World Vision, International Justice Mission and more. How different do you think the world would be today if the church did not exist?

QUESTION 3: The reading for Day 34 provides six images of the church: a building, a body, a family, an army, a flock and a bride. Which of these images do you like the most? Which do you think is the most important, and why?

QUESTION 4: How has the church most impacted your life? How have you most impacted the church?

READ ACTS 2:42-47.

QUESTION 5: The church described in this passage was dynamic and added people on a daily basis. As you read the description, what do you think made this church so appealing to the people around it? What appeals most to you about this church?

_____

_____

_____

QUESTION 6: What are the benefits of being part of a local church?

_____

_____

_____

_____

QUESTION 7: What are some specific things you can do to be helpful to your church?

_____

_____

_____

_____

GOD QUESTIONS CHALLENGE FOR THE WEEK

As a group, brainstorm at least one way you can bless the church(es) you attend. In your next meeting, plan some specific ways to impact the church.

_____

_____

_____

SHARE TOGETHER

Have each member of your group share a prayer request. Write down each person's request and commit to praying for one another throughout the week.

CLOSE IN PRAYER

WHAT'S THE PURPOSE OF MY LIFE?

OPEN IN PRAYER

CONNECT TOGETHER

ICEBREAKER QUESTION: Did you ever have to assemble or repair something that seemed very complicated? Think of one time when you struggled to put something together (or back together), and share the story.

DISCUSS TOGETHER

READ EPHESIANS 2:10.

QUESTION 1: Restate this verse in your own words. What does the Bible say is our purpose?

READ JOHN 15:1-17.

QUESTION 2: Jesus uses a visual example to illustrate a key point. As you envision a vineyard, how would you describe the relationship between the vine and the branches? How does this illustrate our relationship with Jesus?

_____

_____

_____

_____

QUESTION 3: This passage of Scripture also explains our purpose in life. What is that purpose? How is it explained in these verses? Give some examples of how we can "bear fruit" in this life.

_____

_____

_____

_____

QUESTION 4: In order to bear fruit, Jesus tells us we must "abide" or "remain" (depending on your Bible translation) in Him. List some ways in which you can "abide" or "remain" in Jesus.

_____

_____

_____

_____

QUESTION 5: In verses 7 and 16, there is a promise. What is it? There is also a condition for that promise; what is the condition? In the two columns below, give examples of what you might ask God for if you were only thinking of yourself. In the next column, give examples of what you might ask for if you were "abiding" or "remaining" in Jesus and wanting to "bear fruit." Which column is Jesus referring to in verses 7 and 16?

ASK FOR MYSELF ONLY	ASK WHILE ABIDING/ REMAINING IN JESUS

READ MARK 12:28-31.

QUESTION 6: What are some ways in which you can love God? As you consider the question and your answer, think about how Jesus' disciples related to Him.

_____

_____

_____

_____

QUESTION 7: Jesus also commands us to love people. Think about how you relate to others, and in the table below, list what you do well when it comes to loving people. In the second column, list the areas in which you need improvement.

LOVING PEOPLE—WHAT I DO WELL	LOVING PEOPLE—WHERE I CAN IMPROVE

GOD QUESTIONS CHALLENGE FOR THE WEEK

Write a purpose statement for your life. (See Day 36 for an example and some tips.) Once your statement is complete, write two to three steps you can take in the next month to carry out your purpose.

_____

_____

_____

_____

_____

_____

SHARE TOGETHER

Have each member of your group share a prayer request. Write down each person's request and commit to praying for one another throughout the week.

CLOSE IN PRAYER

END NOTES

INTRODUCTION TO SMALL GROUPS

1. Bob Stromberg. "Why Geese Fly Father Than Eagles," (Los Angeles: Big Idea, 2000.)
2. Allen P. Ross, *The Expositor's Bible Commentary, Volume 5, ed.* Frank E. Gaebelein (Grand Rapids, MI: Zondervan, 1991) 907.

The God Questions
Gift Edition

SHARE *THE GOD QUESTIONS*
WITH FRIENDS AND FAMILY!

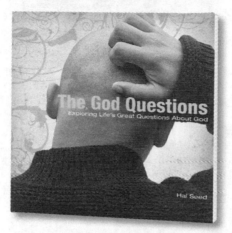

The book features color pages with illustrations, charts and clear-cut, logical answers to these key questions:

- Is God Real?
- Is the Bible True?
- Do All Roads Lead to Heaven?
- How Can a Good God Allow Suffering?

Look for *The God Questions* Gift Edition at your local **Christian Bookstore** or visit **Outreach.com** for bulk quantities.

Jonah: Responding to God in All the Right Ways

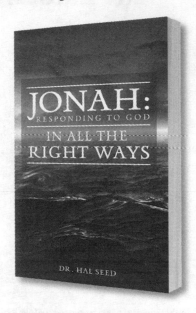

In the story of Jonah, everyone and everything responds to God in amazing ways—except Jonah. Find out how to respond to a God who is both great and gracious to winds and waves, sailors and Ninevites and even to a wayward prophet.

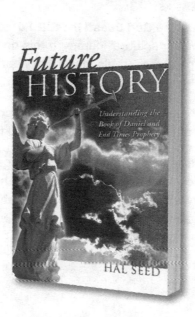

WE'D LIKE TO HEAR FROM YOU

We published *The God Questions* **Gift Edition** to help people with their spiritual journey. If this book (or a particular chapter) has helped you, we would love to hear your story!

Also, if you have questions, we would be happy to connect you with people and resources that can help you find answers.

Please send your comments and experiences with *The God Questions* **Gift Edition** to us through the "Contact Us" button at www.halseedbooks.com. The website also has articles, additional resources and a blog you might enjoy.

ABOUT THE AUTHOR

Dr. Hal Seed pastors New Song Community Church in Oceanside, CA, one of the most innovative and evangelistically effective churches of our day. Hal and his wife Lori have two children, Bryan and Amy, and love helping people find answers to their questions about God. Hal speaks widely on leadership, church planting, personal growth and evangelism. He also writes books that help pastors reach their communities. You can reach him through **www.halseedbooks.com**.